Struggle and strife on a Mayo estate, 1833–1903

To Mar
Wet ~

GW00729137

Richard Kelly

Maynooth Studies in Local History

SERIES EDITOR Raymond Gillespie

This volume is one of five short books published in the Maynooth Studies in Local History series in 2014. Like their predecessors they range widely, both chronologically and geographically, over the local experience in the Irish past. Chronologically they span the world of the medieval priory at Fore to the labour movement in Derry at the beginning of the twentieth century and geographically from Cork to Derry and from Mayo to Meath. Socially they move from the working people of Derry through the emerging medical professionals in Cork to the landlord worlds of Charles Tisdall and the Nolans of Logboy. In doing so they demonstrate the vitality of the study of local history in Ireland and reveal the range of possibilities open to anyone interested in studying the local past. Those possibilities involve the dissection of the local experience in the complex and contested social worlds of which it is part. Such studies of local worlds over such long periods are vital for the future since they not only stretch the historical imagination but provide a longer perspective on the evolution of local societies in Ireland and help us to understand more fully the complex evolution of the Irish experience. These works do not simply chronicle events relating to an area within administrative or geographically determined boundaries, but open the possibility of understanding how and why particular regions had their own personality in the past. Such an exercise is clearly one of the most exciting challenges for the future.

Like their predecessors these five short books are reconstructions of the socially diverse worlds of the poor as well as the rich, women as well as men and reconstruct the way in which those who inhabited those worlds lived their daily lives, often little affected by the large themes that dominate the writing of national history. In addressing these issues, studies such as those presented in these short books, together with their predecessors, are at the forefront of Irish historical research and represent some of the most innovative and exciting work being undertaken in Irish history today. They also provide models that others can follow up and adapt in their own studies of the Irish past. In such ways will we understand better the regional diversity of Ireland and the social and cultural basis for that diversity. They, with their predecessors, convey the vibrancy and excitement of the world of Irish local history today.

Maynooth Studies in Local History: Number 116

Struggle and strife on a Mayo estate, 1833–1903
The Nolans of Logboy and their tenants

Michael Kelly

FOUR COURTS PRESS

Set in 10pt on 12pt Bembo by
Carrigboy Typesetting Services for
FOUR COURTS PRESS LTD
7 Malpas Street, Dublin 8, Ireland
www.fourcourtspress.ie
and in North America for
FOUR COURTS PRESS
c/o ISBS, 920 N.E. 58th Avenue, Suite 300, Portland, OR 97213

ISBN 978–1–84682–518–7

Printed in Ireland
by SprintPrint, Dublin.

Contents

Acknowledgments

I wish to express my sincere thanks to the many people, too numerous to mention individually, who assisted me while I was researching my MA thesis on which this short book is based.

I am most grateful to the editor, Professor Raymond Gillespie, for inviting me to contribute to this series. He and his colleagues in the Department of History at NUI Maynooth have been inspirational in delivering the MA in Local History programme. I thank my fellow students in the class of 2011–12 for their camaraderie and willingness to share ideas and expertise.

I am especially indebted to my thesis supervisor, Dr Gerard Moran, for his insightful advice and patient guidance throughout and for generously sharing with me his deep knowledge of 19th-century Ireland. Canon Kieran Waldron, who first kindled my interest in local history in St Patrick's College, Ballyhaunis, many moons ago, was kind enough to review and comment on the draft text. My research was greatly facilitated by the ever-helpful staff of the following libraries and repositories: John Paul II Library NUI Maynooth, National Archives of Ireland, National Library of Ireland, Registry of Deeds, Valuation Office, Dublin City Archives and Blanchardstown Library.

A special word of thanks for their support is due to my own family and to the extended Waldron family, who first welcomed me to Logboy, the Co. Mayo district at the heart of this study.

My biggest debt is to my wife, Valerie, who not only indulged my pursuit of this time-consuming project but also provided encouragement and constructive criticism along the way.

The front cover illustration is from a sketch by Aloysius O'Kelly of the opening of the new land court in Claremorris which appeared in the *Illustrated London News* of 26 November 1881.

Introduction

In the early hours of Friday, 18 November 1881, a middle-aged father of four was shot dead near his home at Logboy, a small rural community situated midway between the towns of Ballyhaunis and Irishtown in Co. Mayo. The victim, Luke Dillon, was a local tenant farmer who also served as bailiff over the Logboy estate of John Nolan Ferrall. His murder sent shock waves through the community and made national and international news at a time when agrarian outrages were commonplace. It proved to be the catalyst for the landlord's decision to abandon Logboy shortly afterwards and to decamp to Dublin, where he died in 1895. Within a decade of Nolan Ferrall's death, his former tenants had signed agreements to purchase the estate, thus ending the centuries-long reign of the Nolan family as landlords of Logboy.

This short study seeks to trace and analyse the changing fortunes of landlord and tenant on this small estate over the course of the entire Victorian era. Generally speaking, we know more about the lives of the landlords than those of their tenants, especially in the earlier years. Beginning with the stewardship of the previous landlord in the pre-Famine years, the study charts seven decades of struggle and social upheaval during which landlord power was gradually usurped and the aim of tenant ownership of the land – or, in the contemporary phrase, 'a peasant proprietary' – was finally achieved following the three-phased Land War between 1879 and 1903. Nolan Ferrall, who published his own radical proposals for implementing 'a peasant proprietary', did not live to see it materialize.

During the 19th century, the vast majority of Irish people belonged to landed estate communities, of which there were some 7,000 of varying size.[1] Not surprisingly, therefore, the historiography of this period in Irish history is dominated by land-related issues and events, notably the Great Famine and the Land War, with landlord-tenant relations a recurring theme. Yet despite the profusion of local studies and family histories in recent decades, relatively few in-depth studies of individual estates during this turbulent period have been published and most of these deal with larger estates, such as the Lansdowne estate in Co. Kerry, the Gore Booth estate in Co. Sligo, the Leslie estate in Co. Monaghan and the Headfort estates in counties Cavan and Meath. One study based on a single land agency archive has shed light on landlord-tenant relations across several large Irish estates in the 1840s.[2]

Landlords in 19th-century Ireland, although not a homogenous group by any means, have popularly been portrayed as a cruel and rack-renting class who, especially during the Famine, evicted and abandoned their helpless tenants to starvation or emigration. Folk memory of estate clearances by notorious landlords such as Lords Leitrim, Lucan and Clanricarde contributed to this negative stereotype, which was reinforced by influential works by Pomfret and Hooker in the 1930s that held sway right up to the 1970s.[3] Less well-remembered are those benevolent landlords who tried to improve their tenants' lot and promote the general welfare of their neighbourhoods, such as the 'recklessly generous' John Hamilton of Co. Donegal.[4]

Since the 1970s there has been a more nuanced approach to the depiction of Irish landlords and the old stereotype has been largely discarded, at least by historians.[5] Solow (1971) concluded that tenants had not, in fact, been exploited after the Famine since their rents did not even keep pace with agricultural prices.[6] Likewise, Donnelly's study of Co. Cork (1975) argued that the traditional view of landlords as capricious and rack-renting was unjustified.[7] Vaughan's wide-ranging analysis (1994),[8] although not without its critics,[9] further debunked the Pomfret and Hooker orthodoxy by showing that rents were generally moderate, tenure was secure provided rents were paid, and evictions were quite rare, even if landlords were indeed often guilty of incompetent management and failure to invest in their estates. Norton's study (2006) of the land agency of Stewart and Kincaid and the group of landlords it represented concluded that their treatment of tenants was 'both progressive and humane' in the 1840s.[10] Yet Curtis, in highlighting the brutality of evictions, has cautioned that 'in the revisionist rush to acquit the landed proprietors' the impact of the mere threat of eviction on vulnerable tenants can all too easily be overlooked.[11]

An Irish landlord and his tenants may have shared the same geographic space but they inhabited very different worlds. Invariably the landlord's world is the better documented, even in the absence of estate or family papers. Thus, for example, it was found possible by relying mainly on wills and deeds to construct a pedigree of the Nolan landlord family going back to the 16th century (an abridged version is given in the appendix) while their tenants remain largely invisible to historians of the same period. While the lack of estate papers, as in the case of the Logboy estate, is often a deterrent to researching individual estates, it is not necessarily an insurmountable problem given the many alternative and complementary sources,[12] which digitization is increasingly making more accessible and user-friendly. In researching the history of rural parishes, the evidence 'is nearly always absent, fragmentary or ambiguous', as Fowler and Blackwell observed in an English context, but, on the other hand, posing different questions can lead the historian to different evidence: 'basically what you ask is the sort of history that you get'.[13]

A wide range of primary sources is relied on in the present study, the main classes being newspapers, parliamentary papers, contemporary guides and reports, maps, estate rentals, census reports, poor law union minutes books, school records, police reports and petty sessions records. An extensive study like this, requiring the identification, marshalling and analysis of a wide range of sources, can be more challenging than an intensive study based on a cache of estate papers or other ready-made source. One needs to be conscious of the strengths and weaknesses of each source. Newspapers, for example, are a rich source of information but one must be alert to possible editorial bias. For example, during the Land War the *Connaught Telegraph* was edited by James Daly, who was himself a prominent land agitation promoter.

The first chapter of the present study takes stock of the Logboy estate on the eve of the Famine when a rapidly expanding population was eking out a precarious existence on ever-smaller holdings and when emigration, both seasonal and permanent, was on the rise. The estate, the patrimony of the Catholic Nolan family since the 17th century, was inherited by Edmond J. Nolan, a Dublin-based attorney, in 1833, coincidentally the year in which the Logboy tenants first emerge from historical anonymity by being named in an official record. The chapter examines Nolan's role as a paternalistic, albeit largely absentee landlord in supporting the community by financing a new school and church and providing food aid in times of 'distress' and it traces how the estate, like many others of the time, became heavily indebted and ended up in chancery.

The second chapter sketches the impact of the Famine in the locality when, with the indebted estate now under the control of a receiver, the landlord was effectively redundant and the burden of helping the starving populace fell on the parish priest. It establishes that the estate population was decimated during the Famine decade and that the beleaguered landlord was eventually forced to sell the estate through the encumbered estates court. The purchaser was his nephew, John Nolan Ferrall, a barrister based mainly in Dublin or abroad. The chapter looks at Nolan Ferrall's lifestyle and property transactions and how his fortunes waxed and waned into the 1870s.

The third chapter reveals that it was on the Logboy estate that organized land agitation first occurred in response to a confluence of misfortunes which brought Mayo tenants back into poverty in the late 1870s. It considers the role of the Land League and Fenian activists as well as the clergy, the links with agitation at nearby Irishtown, the landlord's own proposals in 1879 for a peaceful transition to 'a peasant proprietary', and finally the deterioration in relations between landlord and tenant culminating in confrontation, evictions and the murder of the estate bailiff at the end of 1881.

The fourth and final chapter investigates the impact of the later phases of the Land War at Logboy. It shows how the landlord was pressurized during the Plan of Campaign in 1887 to concede a rent reduction, one of at least 20 Mayo landlords so targeted. The estate was again in debt by the time of the landlord's death in 1895. The chapter concludes with a look at the role of the United Irish League in campaigning on behalf of the tenants until the Wyndham Land Act of 1903 finally enabled them to become landowners.

A basic aim of this study is to reveal how a small, Catholic-owned estate community evolved over a traumatic period of Irish history. Local perspectives are important in informing our understanding of history at the national level,[14] and may even pinpoint anomalies not revealed in national histories. They also help to build up a clearer and more integrated picture of the history of districts and counties, and encourage comparative studies so that local and regional differences can be established more clearly.[15] Ideally, as Curtis has suggested, the study of landlordism in Ireland requires an aggregate approach, building on case studies of small- and medium-sized estates as well as those of the better-documented large estates.[16] It is hoped that this modest case-study, though barely scratching the surface of the history of a particular place and period, will serve as a building-block in that enterprise.[17]

1. Prelude to disaster: the Logboy estate, 1833–44

When Edmond J. Nolan inherited the family seat in Co. Mayo on the death of his father in 1833, he must have welcomed it as a mixed blessing. A 43-year-old widower with three young children, Nolan was long settled in Dublin where he and his brother Patrick operated a legal practice. His inheritance, a country mansion on 1,400 acres of mixed-quality land, was situated an uncomfortable two-day journey away at Logboy, a rural backwater near where counties Mayo, Roscommon and Galway meet (fig. 1).

While land ownership might well enhance his social standing, Nolan would be hard pressed, owing to the prevailing economic downturn, to extract sufficient rental income from the estate to break even, let alone turn a profit.[1] Moreover the estate, like so many others, came burdened with debt arising from earlier family settlements.[2] There is a perception that landlord extravagance in the 19th century was at the root of their tenants' problems but in reality expenditure on 'the paraphernalia of gentility' was insignificant compared with the cost of charges accumulated from earlier marriage settlements. In fact, the actual operating costs of an estate, including money spent on improvements, accounted for a relatively small proportion of the annual rental, in some cases less than 15 per cent.[3] Nevertheless, under the rules of succession whereby an estate was entailed to the eldest male heir, Edmond Nolan had little choice but to carry on the long line of Nolan custodians of Logboy stretching back to the 17th century.[4]

Relocating permanently to his ancestral home in Co. Mayo was never a realistic option for Edmond Nolan and in 1837 he was still living at Wood View, a villa near Donnybrook, Co. Dublin.[5] While Logboy was recorded as his residence in 1838,[6] the local parish priest, in his grant application for a new school at Logboy that year, confirmed that there was no resident gentleman in the locality; Edmond Nolan, the local landlord backing the school project, was based in Dublin as were his brothers, Patrick and Henry, who were to act as school trustees.[7] However, Edmond must have spent some periods in residence at Logboy House since he was empanelled as a member of the grand jury for Co. Mayo in 1836 and 1838.[8] He had obviously maintained the family links with the Mayo gentry because in 1833 he acted as a character witness for a Mayo magistrate, St Clair O'Malley, in the latter's libel action against the editor of a local newspaper.[9] Also, his late wife was of Mayo stock; he had wed Mary Jane Burke, daughter of John Burke of Ballynew, Castlebar, in August 1823 when he was 33 and she was 19. Their first child, John, was born in December 1825, to be followed by Thomas in 1829. Tragically, Mary Jane died giving birth to their third child, Edmond Jr, in 1830.[10]

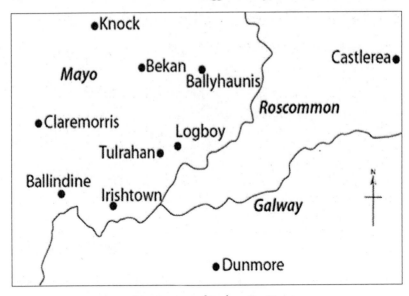

1 Location map of Logboy, Co. Mayo

While there is a dearth of information about life on individual estates in the first half of the 19th century, especially on smaller ones such as Logboy, we can construct a reasonable impression of what it was like by drawing on our knowledge of local and regional happenings. Invariably the gentry are better recorded than the peasantry. At Logboy, in common with much of the west of Ireland, the new landlord would have found a densely populated communal settlement pattern that had developed around partnership leases and the rundale system of strip cultivation.[11] Almost 60 per cent of the land of Co. Mayo was still held in common or joint tenancy even a decade later.[12] The cottages of the tenant partners in a lease were usually grouped in a cluster, known locally as a 'village' or *baile* but now commonly termed a 'clachan'.[13] The presence of clachans in the vicinity of Logboy is confirmed by Bald's map which was surveyed around 1813 and, to a lesser extent, by the first Ordnance Survey map of 1839. Bald's map, for example, shows a cluster of some 30 buildings in the townland of Carrickacat on the Nolan estate.[14] A clachan typically held 10 to 20 partners, according to Archbishop Kelly of Tuam in his evidence to an inquiry on 'the state of Ireland' in 1825;[15] but it expanded organically as the number of holdings increased through subdivision. The neighbours in a clachan, who often had ties of kinship, co-operated with one another in farming tasks such as harvesting, as Isaac Weld observed on his tour of nearby Roscommon in the early 1830s.[16] The cohesion within the clachans, however, was often matched by rivalry between them, finding expression in faction fights on fair days and other occasions of public assembly. Well into the 19th century, Tulrahan at the western end of the Logboy estate was the venue for an annual pattern famed for its faction fights.[17] The clachans were also ready-made units for organizing rent protests or resisting evictions.[18]

The potato crop, cultivated cheaply in ridges on marginal land, was crucial to the rapid evolution of this settlement pattern from the late 18th century. The yield from ridges, or lazy beds, was three times greater than from horse-ploughed drills and while spade cultivation was far more labour-intensive, there was a plentiful supply of cheap labour as the population grew.[19] The nutritious potato crop made it possible for families to subsist on ever-smaller acreages, thereby allowing holdings to be continuously subdivided to enable the tenants' children to marry younger and raise their own families. Housing and fuel, the other essentials for survival, were readily available. Primitive mud-cabins could easily be constructed using local materials while the tenants had access to cheap fuel in the form of peat.

Thus, despite the economic downturn after the battle of Waterloo, the Irish population continued to grow spectacularly, peaking at an estimated 8.7 million by mid-1846,[20] an astonishing 80 per cent increase in the space of half a century.[21] It is reasonable to assume that the population of the Nolan estate evolved in line with the general trend. By 1841 there were at least 670 people living on the estate, in 129 households.[22] This spectacular population growth was, however, marred by periodic hardship or 'distress', often caused by the effects of bad weather on crop and peat harvest yields. Apart from being weather-dependent, the potato crop had two other drawbacks as a food staple. Not only was transport difficult and expensive but, more importantly, potatoes were perishable within a year. Shortages regularly occurred in late summer between the end of the old season's crop and the beginning of the new, a problem that would become particularly acute at Logboy in the early 1840s.

If agricultural productivity was hindered by ever-shrinking holdings and insecurity of tenure, it was exacerbated by farm fragmentation. It was customary to divide up a townland according to the quality of the land, for example, arable, grazing and bog, and then allocate a strip of each quality to every partner in the lease, thus generating a patchwork of plots that inevitably gave rise to border disputes. The legacy of this fragmentation on the Nolan estate is evident, for example, in the layout of farms in the townland of Cossallagh as revealed in the map accompanying the 1851 rental.[23] Some 50 years later, the Congested Districts' Board would still be combatting 'the pernicious system of rundale' in dividing the Dillon estate, the largest in the vicinity of Logboy.[24]

The year that Edmond Nolan inherited the estate also happens to be the year in which at least some of his Logboy tenants came to be identified individually for the first time in an official record, namely the Tithe Applotment Books. The Tithe Applotment Books for the civil parish of Annagh, which included Logboy, detailed the levies payable by Nolan's tenants to the Established Church, the Church of Ireland.[25] However, they did not reflect the full reality on the ground.

Only the heads of households were recorded and some families were not captured at all since one tenant often represented a group, reflecting the old partnership arrangements that still survived in Logboy at that time. Thus, for example, in the townland of Cossallagh comprising 204 acres, only two of Edmond Nolan's tenants, Michael Murphy and Pat Cleary, are named,[26] whereas the census taken eight years later records 62 residents. Census enumeration had commenced in 1813 but did not produce information at townland level until 1841 when, for the first time, a reasonably accurate figure for the total population of the estate becomes available. The census revealed that 670 persons were living in the nine townlands making up the estate, a population density of 2.08 persons per acre with an average of five people in each house (Table 1).[27] Recording of baptisms in Annagh parish did not begin for another decade.[28]

Table 1. Census data for the Logboy estate, 1841

Townland	Acres	Pop.	Houses
Carrickacat	197	114	22
Cartron	88	43	8
Cornacarta	184	99	16
Cossallagh	204	62	17
Largan	104	96	24
Lugboy Demesne	245	36	5
Pollacappul	111	65	9
Redhill	215	82	15
Tulrohaun	47	73	13
Totals	**1,395**	**670**	**129**

Many contemporary observers attributed the problems of Irish agriculture to indolence and incompetence on the part of the tenants, a view that has been challenged by historians.[29] Some Mayo landlords like Thomas Linsay of Hollymount appreciated the value of education in helping tenants to better themselves. Basic educational provision was spreading by 1833, he reported, and young people were benefiting from 'the enlightenment that a little education gives a human being'.[30] Others undoubtedly saw literacy as opening the door to the spread of subversive ideas but Edmond Nolan shared the views of Linsay. When Nolan succeeded at Logboy, the only educational opportunities available to his tenants' children were provided by the fee-based and primitive 'hedge schools', five of which were operating in the locality within the previous decade, suggesting a considerable demand for education despite the poverty.[31] The only 'proper school' in the neighbourhood was located five-and-a-half miles away.[32] The situation was about to improve as a result of initiatives by both the State and the landlord.

Two years earlier the National Education Board had been set up with the power to give grants for the building of new schools. With the backing of the new landlord, who donated a free site within the demesne, the Logboy tenants quickly set about building a school to accommodate 280 pupils, 150 boys and 130 girls. In 1839, they applied to the Board for a grant of two-thirds of the cost, the landlord being willing to advance one-third. Because of 'extreme poverty' and the extra burden of building a church, they could not provide funding themselves.[33] A building grant of £63 was duly awarded in 1839, with local aid amounting to £40.[34] Building of the school must have proceeded in 1838 since it appears on the 1839 Ordnance Survey map. The commissioners' report for 1842 is the first to confirm that Logboy school was in operation, although no teacher's salary had yet been awarded. The same situation pertained in 1843[35] and in 1844.[36] It must be borne in mind that Archbishop McHale of Tuam was vehemently opposed to the British-imposed system of National Schools and from 1840 many of these schools were, following his diktat, being closed again or, as seems to have happened at Logboy, 'being placed, by way of subterfuge, under the management of a competent lay-person, often a local Catholic landlord'.[37]

The renewed confidence of Catholicism in Ireland after Emancipation in 1829 found expression in a wave of church building. Edmond Nolan belonged to a staunch Catholic family and he was sympathetic when the need for a new church to replace the crumbling edifice at Tulrahan came to his attention. He agreed to provide a site but the one he chose proved controversial. The existing church at Tulrahan was in the centre of the half-parish while the new site, at the north-eastern extremity of the estate close to Logboy House, was inconvenient for many people, as well as being low-lying and surrounded by bog and marsh. The parish priest, Fr Coyne, suggested an alternative site west of Logboy but the landlord rejected it.[38] However, construction of an unusual cut-stone church (fig. 2) was already under way by 1839, mainly using limestone sourced in a local quarry, and despite the misgivings about the location, the landlord's generosity in providing a free site together with the 'munificent gift of £280' towards the construction cost was publicly acknowledged.[39] The site lease agreement reserved to the Nolans 'a pew or private seats sufficient to accommodate themselves and their families in the best and most convenient situation in said church'. It also prohibited the use of the church or its grounds for burials.[40]

The church and school projects were scarcely completed when the Logboy tenants were again reminded of their fragile dependence on the potato crop. Their desperate plight in the late summer of 1840 is revealed in the course of a speech by Robert D. Browne MP at a Repeal function in Ballinasloe in November of that year, when he reported what he had heard from his friend Edmond Nolan of Logboy, whom he described as 'a gentleman highly distinguished for the services, as a landlord, which he had rendered to his people'. In supplying Indian meal to 'the starving peasantry of Logboy' that summer, Nolan had often seen them 'retire behind the hedge and eat the raw grain so near to the brink of death

2 St Mary's RC church, Logboy,
built *c.*1840

had starvation brought them'.[41] Indian meal, colloquially known as 'Peel's
brimstone', was both difficult and dangerous to eat if not properly cooked,
because the flint-hard grain could pierce the intestinal wall. However, few people
at that time knew how to cook it properly, even if they had the fuel to do so.[42]
By the late summer of 1842, the Logboy tenants were again desperately short of
food. In October the landlord contributed £5 for the relief of those 'labouring
under sickness and diseases brought on by the starvation which they endured
during the last summer'.[43] In the midst of this distress for his tenants, there was
a happy event for the landlord. On 3 August 1842, Edmond Nolan married for a
second time. His new bride was Barbara Irwin, daughter of Edward Irwin,
Leabeg, Co. Roscommon, and the wedding took place at her mother's house in
Great Brunswick Street, Dublin.[44] Undoubtedly a handsome dowry would have
been a welcome boost to Nolan, who was struggling financially by this time.

In common with thousands of their neighbours, Logboy men were now
making the annual pilgrimage to harvest work in England to earn cash to pay the
rent. This pattern of seasonal migration was already well established in the 1830s,[45]
with up to 90 per cent of adult males travelling in some districts by the 1840s.[46]
In 1841, the heaviest seasonal migration of Irish labourers was from Co. Mayo
when over a third of the population went to work as harvesters.[47] Meanwhile,
permanent emigration was serving as a safety valve on the demographic pressure.
Since 1815, well over one-and-a-half million people had left the country for
good.[48] Most went to North America,[49] but new settlers were also being attracted
to Australia by means of a bounty scheme that operated from 1835 to 1841. At
least two young men from Logboy availed of this scheme; John Cline and James
O'Donnel were both aged 21 years and unmarried when they arrived in New
South Wales on 26 July 1841.[50]

Edmond Nolan became heavily mortgaged and also 'dropped much money in lawsuits', according to his grandson. In addition to Logboy, he had also inherited nearly 1,200 acres of land in south Co. Sligo. At some time after 1838, he appears to have indulged in land speculation by purchasing almost 1,000 acres formerly owned by Capt. Henry Browne in Killasser parish, some 20 miles from Logboy.[51] Subsidizing the building of the new church and school at Logboy had been a further drain on his resources. He was soon struggling to retain ownership of his properties because of the increasing burden of the yearly charges.[52] To make matters worse, the legal practice which he operated with his brother, Patrick, was also owed money by Patrick's brother-in-law, Daniel H. Ferrall of Beechwood, Co. Roscommon. Although Ferrall was one of the biggest landowners in Co. Roscommon and apparently wealthy with a gross annual rental income of over £9,000, his estates, just like the Nolan estate, were encumbered with a heavy debt burden from his predecessors.[53] He had also suffered certain financial embarrassments since the early 1820s and had been the target of an investigation into the office of sheriff in 1825 in the course of which Edmond Nolan, as his attorney, had been questioned about alleged improper payments by Ferrall to the sheriff's offices in Dublin and Roscommon in return for leniency in the execution of warrants against him.[54] Eventually, in the 1840s, Ferrall absconded to Paris and London in order to evade his creditors, including the law firm of E. and P. Nolan.[55]

Although Edmond Nolan was listed as clerk of the crown for Co. Sligo in 1842 with an address at 3 Inns Quay, Dublin,[56] he lived abroad for a period in the 1840s. One surmises that his move abroad was prompted by health and lifestyle considerations rather than the desire to evade creditors; nevertheless there is evidence of increasing financial pressures on him at this time. He returned to Ireland in 1846 to deal with an embarrassing court case, Burke v Crean, concerning certain convoluted financial transactions. The defendant, Crean, had been accommodating the Nolans by signing blank acceptances that were afterwards drawn by Edmond Nolan and cash obtained from various parties, including the plaintiff Burke, who resorted to legal action to have the acceptances honoured after Crean claimed that they were not genuine. Edmond Nolan appeared as a witness for Burke and both he and his brother, Patrick, gave evidence that the acceptances were indeed genuine. He told the court that he was in a 'most painful' position in having to prove a debt that was, in effect, 'incurred for his accommodation'. Eventually, a settlement was reached with Nolan undertaking to pay off the debt by instalments. Interestingly, both the presiding judge and counsel for the plaintiff took great pains to avoid any insinuation of wrongdoing on Nolan's part.[57]

Edmond Nolan engaged in various legal manoeuvres 'to protect himself against the pressure of mortgages and meet bad times', arranging to have the estate vested at different times in one or other of his two sons, John and Thomas, although ultimately it was the former who would inherit.[58] On the eve of the Famine, landlord indebtedness was commonplace and many estates, particularly the smaller ones like Logboy, were on the verge of bankruptcy.[59] The collection of rent was a constant difficulty.[60] Because of the complications of title arising from family settlements, it was easier to encumber an estate than to sell it.[61] In the Swinford district alone, for example, no fewer than nine encumbered properties were being administered by the court of chancery at this time.[62] By 1844, a total of 874 Irish estates were being administered by court-appointed receivers,[63] and the Logboy estate was one of these.[64] Appointment of a receiver was likely to have serious repercussions for the tenants, often leading to 'a deterioration in cultivation and in the condition of the people'.[65] A receiver had no personal interest in the condition of the tenantry;[66] his role was simply to collect money and in the process he often 'extorted, evicted and distrained the tenants'.[67]

When the mantle of landlord of Logboy had passed to Edmond Nolan in 1833, there were already signs of more difficult days ahead both for him and his tenants. Living in clustered villages and precariously dependent on a single food crop, the tenants were at the mercy of frequent occurrences of hunger and disease. The Poor Inquiry of 1835 had produced the sobering statistic that up to two-and-a-half million Irish people were 'in severe want' for the greater part of each year.[68] The increasing hardship being experienced by the tenants is reflected in the upward trend in the death rate in Co. Mayo: an increase of 4.3 per cent in 1843 and 8.3 per cent in 1844.[69] To generate cash to pay the rent, tenants were increasingly forced to migrate seasonally to farm work in England and Scotland. Permanent emigration was also growing for those who had the means. Whether Edmond Nolan actually encouraged and assisted emigration to alleviate the demographic pressure, as some landlords like Sir Robert Gore Booth did,[70] is a moot point.

The problems facing Mayo landlords and tenants on the eve of the Famine were summed up in the evidence given to the Devon Commission in January 1844 by William Sherrard, a land agent who managed properties in several counties including Mayo. All estates, he said, were 'suffering from a super-abundant population'. He believed that there was considerable scope for land improvement but only if tenants were granted 21-year leases. The Logboy tenants all held their holdings from year to year, with the exception of Theobald Dillon, who was tenant for life.[71] Sherrard regarded the constant subdividing of land and establishing of families on four-acre farms as the insidious problem. It would inevitably lead 'to the rapid increase of a pauper and starving population, and, consequently, to the decreased value of the property'.[72] He could scarcely have contemplated the scale of the catastrophe that lay ahead.

Edmond Nolan also seems to have been less than prudent in managing his own finances. His rental income had obviously suffered for many years because of economic circumstances outside his control but he also fared badly in certain lawsuits and in some ill-judged property speculation. By 1845, the Logboy estate was under the control of the court of chancery and the landlord, now residing overseas, was effectively out of the picture. The Logboy tenants, whose survival was precariously reliant on the yield of a single crop and who were now at the mercy of the receiver, had little reason to be optimistic about the future.

2. The Great Famine and its aftermath, 1845–75

On Sunday 12 October 1845, 'upwards of 200,000' people converged on Castlebar in driving rain to welcome the charismatic Repeal campaigner, Daniel O'Connell. Whether any Logboy tenants made the arduous 20-mile journey to catch a glimpse of the ageing Liberator is not recorded but their pastor, Fr Eugene Coyne, was among 500 dignitaries who attended a banquet in his honour that evening. Sheltered from the elements in a specially erected pavilion behind Flynn's hotel, the guests enjoyed excellent food and wines, 'including champagnes, sherry, and port … of the oldest vintage and choicest selection'.[1] While this lavish fare was being served up, alarm bells were already sounding locally about an impending food crisis.

In mid-November, the parish priest of Claremorris, Fr James Hughes, described the devastating progress of potato blight in a letter to his friend and fellow Claremorris-man, John Gray, owner of the *Freeman's Journal*. After celebrating 'a station Mass' in the village of Upper Mace, the priest had witnessed a basket of potatoes being brought in to be cooked; not one of them proved to be edible. He reported that the local landlord, James Browne of Claremount, was so concerned about the potato crisis that he had taken the unusual step of instructing his tenants not to sell their oats,[2] an important cash crop and source of rent money. Without timely aid, Fr Hughes now warned, famine 'with all its awful consequences' was inevitable.

While direct evidence of estate life at Logboy from this period has not survived, the degree of hardship suffered by the tenants can be gauged from contemporary accounts about the wider locality. In Ballyhaunis, the parish town serving Logboy, the price of potatoes in January was up to 60 per cent higher than a year earlier.[3] By August the people of the district were 'not far off starvation' and it was feared that violence would erupt should the government depot be closed.[4] On 17 September, the parish priest, Fr Coyne, himself the holder of a large farm near Logboy, wrote to the lord lieutenant pleading for help: 'If the government were to witness the misery and wretchedness that I daily meet with, they would not be so dilatory in sending substantial relief; the murmuring of these hungry, half-naked persons, often having pawned their clothes to purchase a stone of meal and could not get it, should soften the hardest heart to compassion'.[5]

On 25 September, along with nine local clergymen Fr Coyne again wrote to the lord lieutenant pleading for a food depot for Ballyhaunis 'in the name of our starving parishioners … or else the consequences are likely to be dreadful'.[6] On

3 October, he sent off another plea for help, this time to Sir Randolph Routh of the Relief Commission, pointing out 'the awful state of destitution' in his locality. Many would now be 'rotting in their graves', he said, but for the £130 contributed by local shopkeepers, gentry and clergy for the purchase of Indian meal. 'Unless the government helps', he prophesized, 'the people will die in their hundreds'. On 13 October, he again wrote to Routh to press the request for a food depot, stating that 'meal is now beyond famine prices'.[7] Edmond Nolan, as previously mentioned, returned to Dublin for a period in November 1846 to deal with a court case, but it is not known whether he visited Logboy to see conditions there.

While the suddenness and scale of the food crisis may have caught the authorities unawares, there had been warning signs for more than a decade, notably in the Poor Inquiry of 1835. The government's solution had been to extend the English poor law system to Ireland in 1838. The country was organized into 130 new administrative poor law unions, each one obliged to provide a workhouse for the relief of the destitute poor.[8] The Logboy estate came within the catchment area of the Castlerea union which catered for a population of 85,895 (in 1831) spread over three counties: Roscommon, Galway and Mayo. In March 1846 the O'Conor Don MP told a parliamentary committee that the new workhouse at Castlerea,[9] some 15 miles from Logboy, had been fit to receive paupers since 1843 but it had not yet opened due to lack of funds. The union also had a large debt, he said, owing to difficulty in collecting rates.[10]

By the end of the year, it was obvious that the official response to the famine crisis was totally inadequate, as Archbishop McHale of Tuam pointed out in a scathing letter to Prime Minister Russell on 13 December 1846. He warned that 'the people's bones, "slain by the sword of famine", and piled into cairns more numerous than the ancient pyramids, shall tell posterity the ghastly triumphs of your brief but disastrous administration'.[11] Fr Hughes of Claremorris was equally forthright in his letter of 30 December to the new chief secretary, Henry Labouchere, complaining about the delay in starting public works and paying wages: 'The people of this parish and surrounding districts are starving in multitudes. Already nine have died of starvation and ten times nine are ready to follow them, whose constitutions are irreparably destroyed by hunger. These deaths I pronounce so many murders'.[12]

The 'appalling distress' of the poor of south-east Mayo is graphically illustrated by an incident that occurred near Claremorris in early 1847. A local journalist, hearing a rumour about a poor starving family scavenging a horse carcase, went out to the townland of Killbegwills to investigate. There he met Mrs Kelly, mother of the family in question, who pointed to her six emaciated children and explained tearfully: 'These did not taste a morsel of food for four days. Three of them, we thought, were dying of hunger; but my husband, hearing that Macken's horse had died, brought home a basket full of it, which was all that the dogs had left, and on this alone we have lived the whole week, and the Lord alone knows what I will do now for my starving children since it is gone'.[13]

This was not an isolated incident. A few months later, a traveller en route to Claremorris from Knock encountered two women butchering the hindquarters of a horse carcase in order to salvage some meat for their starving families. Famished women and children were seen picking nettles and watercress – of which the streams and marshes had already been stripped bare.[14] In the parish of Bekan, adjacent to Logboy, an inquest on the body of Michael Cunnane held on 8 December delivered the euphemistic verdict that death was due to 'insufficiency of food'.[15] There were many similar verdicts while many more deaths never came to the coroner's attention. By now, the plight of the Mayo tenants was gaining international notoriety. In June, for example, a donation of £14 was received from the citizens of Burlington, Iowa, for famine relief in Claremorris.[16] Any Logboy tenant who ended up in Castlerea workhouse at this time would have been dismayed by the overcrowding and disease there. In April, the master and matron had both died, the doctor resigned and most of the 990 inmates had fever.[17]

On 17 April 1848, Fr Coyne wrote to the archbishop of Dublin thanking him for sending £15 for famine relief and pleading for more as otherwise hundreds would die of starvation. On his daily rounds, he had seen his people lying on their beds with hunger, fever and dysentery. His parish was 'the worst off of any' in the locality and there was no landlord to help them. Undoubtedly, he had the Nolan estate in mind when he wrote that 'the lands are in chancery and the landlords in some safe hiding place'.[18] In the cash-strapped Castlerea union, the military had been drafted in to enforce poor-rate collection.[19] In the midst of their own distress in 1848, the Logboy tenants learned of a personal tragedy for their absent landlord with the death of his youngest son, 18-year-old Edmond Junior, who was a Jesuit novice at Stonyhurst College in Lancashire.[20]

Due to the notorious Gregory clause, no tenant holding more than a quarter acre of land was eligible for public assistance either in the workhouse or outside it.[21] This provision helped landlords in clearing their estates of the poorest tenants who were facing Hobson's choice: either surrender their holdings or starve. Nevertheless many in Annagh parish held out until the very last moment as Fr Coyne reported in March 1849: 'the poor landowners … are now in a most wretched state without food or seed' but 'they are still not giving up their land lest (as they say) they would never have their own fireside again'.[22] Moreover, tenants regarded entry to the workhouse as the final straw because it relegated them to the status of 'pauper', a new and distinct category of second-class citizen deprived of the basic rights of citizenship through disenfranchisement and loss of personal reputation and freedom.[23]

Fr Coyne was convinced that the death toll from starvation would rise 'from this time to the next harvest' and was likely to exceed that of the three previous years taken together. He reported that the body of a woman was found by the ditch at Culnacleha, adjacent to Logboy House. She had died of starvation. 'If outdoor relief is not immediately given to the landholders and able-bodied, the consequences I fear will be awful', he warned.[24] Some semblance of normality in the vicinity of Logboy is suggested by the fact that the December fair at Tulrahan was advertised, as usual, in the press.[25] On the other hand, it comes as no surprise that Logboy school was suspended that year.[26]

In June 1850, the *Freeman's Journal* challenged an optimistic assessment of the state of the country, citing as evidence a recent event at Claremorris. During a board of guardians' meeting, more than 1,000 people 'literally in a state of nudity' assembled outside in the hope of getting a meal ticket. Only a few succeeded, 'the rest of the ragged multitude departing "to live on hope" or … "the tops of nettles"'.[27] The starving crowd may well have included some of Nolan's impoverished tenants since Logboy now came within the catchment area of the new Claremorris union, formed on 22 February 1850. The Logboy tenants were liable for rents well in excess of the land valuation, although 'considerable abatements' had been granted by the receiver.[28]

While there is little direct evidence of the experiences of individual Logboy tenants during the Great Famine, we can glean some understanding how they fared from a comparison of the census reports of 1841 and 1851. In that period the overall estate population fell by more than 36 per cent, from 670 to 426, although there were very significant differences in the fortunes of the individual townlands.[29] For example, in the small townland of Largan, one of three comprising the estate demesne, there was a dramatic reduction in population from 96 to 25 with a corresponding reduction in the number of inhabited houses from 24 to six. The townland never recovered from this loss of three-quarters of its people and by the end of the century not a single soul remained there.

The rate of population decline for the Logboy estate (36 per cent) was higher than for Co. Mayo overall (29 per cent),[30] and substantially higher than for the parish of Annagh as a whole (24 per cent) or for the adjacent parishes of Kilvine (24 per cent), Aghamore (21 per cent), Kilcolman (21 per cent), Bekan (15 per cent) and Knock (6 per cent). The most likely explanation for this dramatic decline is that the population had been decimated by starvation and famine-related disease, although it is entirely possible that some clachans were cleared in preparation for the sale of the insolvent estate in 1851 since prospective purchasers of encumbered estates generally favoured properties that had been cleared of tenants, or at least of those that were uneconomic.[31]

Of all Irish landowners, those in Co. Mayo were most likely to see the benefits of compulsory clearances. A staggering 75 per cent of Mayo land occupiers had holdings valued at £4 or less, which meant that the landlords had to shoulder almost the entire rates burden.[32] Even the relatively humane marquis of Sligo, swamped with personal debt and dwindling rents, began clearing his Mayo estates of the pauper tenantry in 1848, arguing that it was a question of 'ejecting or being ejected'.[33] Between 1849 and 1854, over 26,000 Mayo tenants were evicted permanently.[34] It is difficult to avoid the conclusion that there must have been a clearance of the demesne lands at Logboy, most likely in preparation for the sale of the estate in 1851. The Ordnance Survey map of 1839 shows little evidence of the 38 houses recorded for the demesne townlands in 1841, suggesting that many of these were not regarded as permanent structures.[35]

Many landlords, finally realizing that their estates needed to be consolidated and the population reduced, came to see 'assisted passage' emigration as the cheapest solution. It saved on the cost of financing relief for starving tenants. The fact that the emigrants' remittances often accrued to the landlord in rent was a bonus.[36] Emigration was a controversial remedy but, as a local newspaper editor remarked, it offered 'the best and most effectual means by which the overgrown and starving mass of our peasantry may escape the impending ruin'.[37] However, the poorer classes, particularly the landless cottiers, were effectively prevented by their lack of resources from availing of the more expensive escape routes, such as the trans-Atlantic crossing.[38] In 1851, the Nolan estate was home to 30 such landless cottiers.[39]

Any Logboy tenants contemplating emigration to North America in 'Black '47' would surely have been discouraged by the horror stories emanating from Quebec, as reported in a Mayo newspaper in July of that year. There were 21,000 passengers queued up at the Grosse-Île immigration station, 900 more had died during the Atlantic crossing and a further 700 expired on arrival. Some 200 burials had taken place on the very day of the report, 5 July. There were 1,500 sick on board the vessels and 1,100 more ill on the island itself.[40] But emigration continued apace. Before 1851, it was mainly family groups rather than individuals who had left.[41] In the parish of Aghamore, a few miles from Logboy, a group of families abandoned their homes around this time and migrated en masse to Yorkshire.[42]

In the case of the Logboy estate there are just a few tantalizing glimpses of emigrant experiences. In 1847, Thomas Murray and several younger siblings abandoned their holding in the townland of Cossallagh for a new life in America. They eventually settled down to farming life in Minnesota, where Thomas died in 1898 at the age of 90.[43] Despite the unhappy circumstances of his emigration, his gravestone bears proud testimony to his Irish roots 'in the town of Logboy, Co. Meyo, Parish of Anack, Ireland'.[44] Having grown up in Logboy long before the school was built, Thomas was probably illiterate, hence the phonetic spellings of his native county and parish on his gravestone. Another Famine-era emigrant from Logboy to America was James Neary who lived in the townland of Culnacleha, which later became part of the Nolan estate. He was a blacksmith who, in March 1847, was described as being 'in tolerable circumstances', which would explain why he was able to pay his passage to America in 1851.[45]

Logboy tenants, as previously mentioned, were well accustomed to seasonal migration to the farms of England for harvest work. Some decided to make the move permanent. In March 1851, Logboy-born John O'Donnel was living in a house at Newnham, Gloucestershire, with his English-born wife and daughter. Also in the house was a relative named Thomas O'Donnel, probably John's brother, with a wife and two young daughters, all Logboy-born; the youngest was only one year old, so the family had obviously arrived in England only

RENTAL
or
THE LOGBOY ESTATE,
SITUATE IN THE BARONY OF COSTELLOE, AND COUNTY OF MAYO, HELD IN FEE,
WHICH WILL BE
Set up and Sold by Public Auction,
At GILL'S HOTEL, in the Town of BALLINASLOE, in the County of GALWAY,
ON TUESDAY, THE 7th DAY OF OCTOBER, 1851,
AT THE HOUR OF ONE O'CLOCK IN THE AFTERNOON,
BY ORDER OF THE COMMISSIONERS FOR THE SALE OF INCUMBERED ESTATES IN IRELAND,
IN LOTS. AS SET FORTH IN THE ANNEXED RENTAL AND PARTICULARS OF SALE.

3 Public auction notice for the Nolan estate at Logboy, 1851

recently. John O'Donnel was employed as an 'excavator' (navvy) while Thomas was a labourer;[46] both were probably working on the extension of the railway towards south Wales. Since O'Donnel was a rare surname in Logboy, it is likely that they were close relatives of James O'Donnel who had emigrated to Australia a decade earlier, and of James O'Donnell who emigrated to Canada, where he died in Vancouver in 1877 aged 64.[47]

A petition for the sale of the Logboy estate was filed on 28 June 1850,[48] the disposal of insolvent landed estates having been authorized by the Encumbered Estates Act of 1849. Previously such sales had been stymied by the fact that most estates were entailed. Now, upon application by a creditor, the encumbered estates court could sell an estate where debts exceeded 50 per cent of yearly income. Once outstanding debts were satisfied, a full legal title to the property was conferred on the purchaser, though no security was given to existing tenants.[49]

The Logboy estate was first offered for sale at a public auction in Gill's hotel, Ballinasloe, on 7 October 1851 (fig. 3). The sale advertisement indicated that the demesne included 80 acres 'tastefully planted with useful and ornamental timber, varying from 30 to 20 years' growth, which tend much to beautify and shelter the ground'. Logboy House itself was 'well sheltered and surrounded by a neatly-planted pleasure ground' and it could, with some outlay, be transformed into 'a commodious residence'.[50] One of the estate townlands, Cossallagh, comprising 11 holdings ranging in size from nine to 30 acres, was said to be 'in the hands of an industrious peasantry'. The estate did not sell on that occasion, however, and the adjourned sale was advertized to take place at the court of the Encumbered Estates' Commissioners in Dublin on 6 July 1852. In fact, the estate did not sell until 1855. In the end, it did not leave the control of the wider Nolan family since the purchaser was the landlord's nephew, John Nolan Ferrall, the only son of Edmond Nolan's brother and business partner, Patrick. He was a barrister with addresses at Beechwood House, Co. Roscommon, and Merrion Square, Dublin. The Ferrall element of his surname came from his mother, Rose Ferrall, who died in 1853, and he had inherited portion of the extensive Roscommon estates of her late brother, Daniel Henry Ferrall, whom we met in the previous chapter.

John Nolan Ferrall was born in 1832 and in line with family tradition he was educated by the Jesuits at Stonyhurst in Lancashire. He was admitted to the King's Inns for training as a barrister in 1852.[51] In 1854, he was living at Upper Fitzwilliam St, Dublin.[52] After acquiring Logboy, he became active in local administration and economic development in Connacht. In March 1856, he was on the committee of the North Western Railway of Ireland, which aimed to connect the seaports of Mayo and Sligo with Dublin and Belfast.[53] In April, he was a member of Claremorris board of guardians.[54] In July 1857 he was sworn in to serve on the grand jury for Mayo,[55] and in November 1858 he was returned as high sheriff for the county.[56] He also maintained his interest in Roscommon politics, speaking at a meeting of the Liberal electors in Elphin in April 1859,[57] and a year later he was appointed a deputy lieutenant for that county,[58] where he had strong family ties. By now Nolan Ferrall was dividing his time between the west of Ireland and Dublin, where he retained a substantial townhouse at 3 Merrion Square West, near another family with Roscommon roots, the Wildes.[59] He improved the Logboy estate, extending the plantation and importing new varieties of trees and shrubs to enhance the pleasure grounds but his attempt to bring a water supply to Logboy House by means of a canal proved unsuccessful.[60] It is likely that he upgraded Logboy House (also known as Lugboy House) which, although no sketch or detailed description of it has come to light, was a substantial mansion which reportedly had 24 rooms with 36 windows at its zenith.[61] The Ordnance Survey map of 1893 (fig. 4) shows that the ground floor area of the house was far greater than that of the church.

Meanwhile, the Logboy estate population slowly began to recover after the decimation of the Famine decade. It climbed by over 6 per cent, from 426 to 453, between 1851 and 1861, reflecting the general economic recovery. The number of inhabited houses did not change in that time so the population increase must be attributed to larger family size rather than more families. The path of economic recovery was not smooth, however. While the Crimean War had temporarily boosted agricultural prices in 1853, another economic depression lasting five years began in 1859. Bad harvests, particularly in 1863–4, once again caused distress and a renewed upsurge in emigration.[62] However, the new landlord of Logboy was quick to respond to this latest crisis for his tenants by granting them a rent abatement of 12½ per cent in the spring of 1863, a gesture that was well received as an example to be followed by other landlords.[63] The population recovery was short-lived, however, and was more than offset during the ensuing two decades. Between 1841 and 1881 the estate population almost halved (Table 2). As mentioned in the previous chapter, the three townlands comprising the estate demesne were virtually wiped out, their total population plummeting from 197 to just 13. There was an even greater reduction in the number of inhabited houses, indicating a degree of consolidation of holdings. Emigration was still increasing. During one week in April 1864, some 650 persons left Mayo by train, more than half of them from Ballyhaunis.[64]

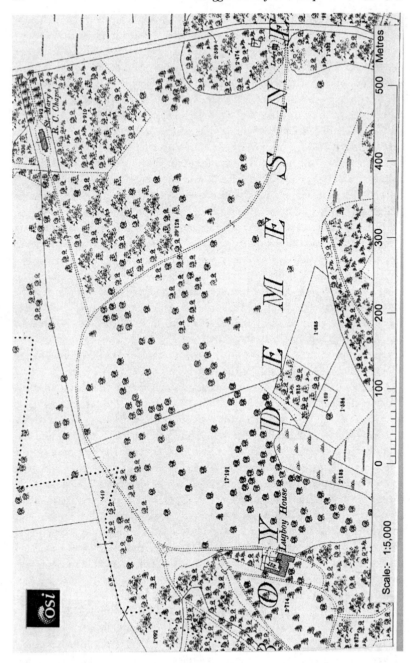

4 Detail of 25" map showing location of Logboy House and St Mary's church, 1893. Ordnance Survey Ireland Permit No. 8932. © Ordnance Survey Ireland/Government of Ireland

Table 2. Estate population by townland at 10 year intervals, 1841–81

Townland	1841	1851	1861	1871	1881
Carrickacat	114	73	107	92	92
Cartron	43	31	24	40	43
Cornacarta	99	64	71	78	61
Cossallagh	62	57	58	56	48
Largan	96	25	12	7	5
Lugboy Demesne	36	22	13	10	8
Pollacappul	65	48	22	8	0
Redhill	82	70	80	71	64
Tulrohaun	73	36	66	41	26
Totals	**670**	**426**	**453**	**403**	**347**

Source: Census of Ireland reports

John Nolan Ferrall was a far more extensive landowner than previous Logboy landlords. Family considerations undoubtedly played a role in his decision to purchase the Logboy estate, which had been something of a millstone round his uncle's neck. Land ownership still 'represented a social summit' in Ireland and land purchase seemed like a sound investment in the context of the post-Famine economic recovery.[65] Nevertheless, Nolan Ferrall and his father, Patrick Nolan, may have over-extended themselves financially in buying up encumbered properties in the 1850s. When Edmond Nolan had been forced to sell his Killasser property of 964 acres in 1852, it was Patrick who snapped it up for £2,500.[66] Nolan Ferrall himself then added to the family's Killasser estate by buying up an adjacent property from the Revd William Jackson in 1853. In 1855, he had also bought 1,735 acres at Rockfield in the parish of Knock, part of the encumbered estate of Lord Oranmore and Brown, who had owed him £1,200. To complete his property transactions, he had borrowed £25,000 from the Standard Life Assurance Company in Britain.[67] The fact that Nolan Ferrall had to put some of his property portfolio up for sale in 1863 suggests that he may have already started to experience difficulties. In December his interest in a small property of 131 acres at Castletana in the parish of Kilbride, Co. Roscommon, was up for sale by order of the landed estate court on his own petition,[68] although it was still unsold four years later. However, by 1867 he was seeking to offload a more substantial property, in addition to the small Roscommon property. This time it was his Killasser estate of 3,606 acres that was put up for sale.[69]

Despite the heavy debt burden he had incurred through investing in land, Nolan Ferrall was somehow able to maintain an extravagant lifestyle into the 1860s. In August 1862, he had left Logboy for continental Europe,[70] and by 1864

5 John Nolan Ferrall's yacht *Red Gauntlet*

he was spending much of his time there, according to evidence that emerged later in a court case.[71] He had also acquired a substantial hunting and fishing retreat, Glendavlough Lodge, west of Lough Conn, Co. Mayo, which boasted 'a portable iron house' imported from Liverpool at a cost of £500 and a well-stocked wine cellar. In August 1863 he hosted some senior legal figures there, including Chief Justice Monahan and Judge Keogh; the latter would become infamous for his judgment in the Galway election petition case of 1872 which saw the unseating of Capt. John Philip Nolan, a cousin of Nolan Ferrall.[72] Like many of his Merrion Square neighbours, Nolan Ferrall also joined the elite yachting set and in September 1863, he was appointed to a committee to make arrangements for the reception and entertainment of Rear-Admiral Dacres and the Channel fleet under his command.[73] In March 1864, his own luxury schooner yacht *Red Gauntlet* (fig. 5)[74] set sail from Kingstown for a Mediterranean cruise,[75] during which the yacht's faulty chronometer had to be repaired at Naples.[76] In August, the yacht left Malta for Constantinople,[77] and in October it departed Valetta for England with just a single passenger, Mr P. Nolan, undoubtedly the owner's father.[78] The following year, Nolan Ferrall was elected a member of the Royal Thames Yacht Club.[79] But this high living could not be sustained and by 1867 the yacht had been sold, eventually passing into the ownership of another wealthy Irish gentleman, Edward Langtry, who used it to woo his future bride, the infamous Lillie Langtry.[80]

Despite long absences, Nolan Ferrall did not lose touch with developments in the west of Ireland. Although he resigned as deputy lieutenant for Roscommon in 1866, he was appointed to the corresponding position for Mayo in March of that year, succeeding Lord Dillon.[81] A year later he was sworn in as a member of the grand panel for the Mayo assizes.[82] He still contributed to local Catholic causes. In 1866, he subscribed £3 to a testimonial fund for the archbishop of Tuam,[83] and in October 1868, he donated £100 towards the new Catholic church at Killasser, where he had extensive property.[84] He maintained social contact with the local gentry, participating in a meeting of the Co. Galway Hounds at Ballyglunin Park in December 1869 in the company of such well-known Galway families as the Persses, Blakes, and O'Kellys.[85]

Nolan Ferrall's days as a playboy bachelor came to an end when, at the age of 37, he married Julia, youngest daughter of his old friend Chief Justice Monahan, at Bray, Co. Wicklow, on 9 August 1869. Julia was a devout Catholic who took a personal interest in the religious instruction of the Logboy children, often teaching catechism on Sundays after Mass and distributing free catechisms.[86] She and her husband went on to have three children. John Cecil, the eldest, was born on 22 November 1875 in Paris, indicating that the family was still spending time overseas. Henry James was born in 1878 and a daughter, Rose, was born at Bray in 1882. None of the three children would marry or have issue and the Nolan Ferrall surname died with them.

While Nolan Ferrall still held a considerable land bank in the mid-1870s, the bulk of which (9,731 acres) was in Co. Mayo,[87] his financial pressures were beginning to mount. Landlords like him who had borrowed heavily after the Famine now experienced a larger proportion of their income being eaten up by interest repayments.[88] He was forced to sell his fishing lodge through the landed estates court in June 1872.[89] He faced further embarrassment a year later when he was sued by bankers Guinness & Mahon in the court of exchequer for the recovery of £1,005 on foot of bills of exchange that he had accepted for the accommodation of his father,[90] who had fled the country 'in embarrassed circumstances' in September 1873 and had not returned.[91] In February 1876, he lost a case in the court of appeal in chancery brought by a Ballina merchant to compel him to perform an agreement of 1869 for the sale of 550 acres at Lahardane. This was another situation where his father, acting as his solicitor, had left him in the lurch.[92] In the meantime, on 3 June 1875, he had sold 282 acres in Co. Mayo through the landed estates court for £4,875.[93]

In the three decades since 1845 the Logboy estate community, landlord and tenant alike, had experienced profound change. Despite the paucity of direct evidence about the impact of the Famine on the estate, we can reasonably conclude, from the available information about the locality, that the tenants' experiences were indeed harrowing. Despite the best efforts of their pastor, Fr Coyne, in pressurizing the authorities to deliver relief measures, the estate lost over one-third of its population during the Famine decade. This dramatic decline must be attributable to death and emigration, with a strong suspicion that some townlands had been virtually cleared, at the behest of the receiver, to facilitate the sale of the estate.

Ironically, the reduction in population pressure brought about by the Famine was one of the factors that provided hope for the Logboy tenants that there were brighter days ahead. Moreover, the signs of price recovery for agricultural produce from 1851 had helped to create a sense of optimism about the future, as did the arrival of a new and apparently well-resourced landlord who showed leniency during the agricultural crisis of the early 1860s, although admittedly the response of tenants generally to that particular crisis had been 'expressed in emigration rather than outrage'.[94] At the same time, the tide was gradually turning against the landlords. Their electoral power had waned since the extension of the franchise in 1850 and, regardless of how well they had previously treated their tenants, they all came to be regarded as the political enemy.[95] The seeds of the subversive idea of 'a peasant proprietary', that tenants themselves rather than landlords were legitimately entitled to the land, had been sown as far back as the Young Ireland movement with its slogan 'the soil of Ireland for the people of Ireland'.[96] It had been encouraged by the breaking of the entail in the Encumbered Estates Act but it would only bear fruit, as we shall see, with the advent of the Land League.

3. Agrarian violence: the Land League years

There is no evidence of agrarian unrest at Logboy during the first two decades of Nolan Ferrall's tenure. However, in the late 1870s a confluence of misfortunes stirred up fears of another Great Famine and mobilized tenants to demand rent reductions and resist threatened evictions.[1] Potato and fodder supplies were drastically diminished by bad weather, cattle prices collapsed due to foreign competition, and poultry were wiped out by cholera.[2] The bad weather also caused a fuel shortage, which no doubt was what prompted two tenants to steal some wood from Logboy demesne in February 1879.[3] Seasonal farm work in Britain, on which many tenants were so reliant, had dried up due to mechanization. This had a devastating impact since seasonal migrants from the Ballyhaunis area would normally expect to earn in a few weeks in England as much as double their annual income at home.[4] On the other hand, some perceptive Mayo landlords, such as Captain Sheffield of Claremorris, were noticing a new brazenness on the part of their tenants in refusing to the pay full rent even if they had the means;[5] they were 'strategic defaulters', in modern parlance. Moreover, the full rent could scarcely have been considered excessive since the rental income on many estates had barely doubled between 1815 and 1875.[6]

The first indication of trouble brewing at Logboy came in early 1879 when 'a mob' attacked Thomas Rogers, a sheriff's bailiff from Ballyhaunis, as he was attempting to serve processes for non-payment of rent on the Nolan Ferrall estate. Rogers had been accompanied by four policemen, so clearly trouble had been anticipated. The RIC's annual return of outrages indicates that this incident occurred on 9 January and that a man named Martin Hopkins was indicted but the case was adjourned after the jury disagreed. On 5 June, according to the same source, Rogers was again attempting to serve processes when a crowd assaulted him with sticks and stones. Charges against John Cleary and Mary Conway arising from this incident were dismissed by the magistrates at the petty sessions.[7] On 1 July, Michael Murphy of Redhill, William Ruane of Carrickacat and Martin Hopkins of Lenamore were charged with unlawfully and riotously assembling 'with divers others' at Lurgan Cross and assaulting Thomas Rogers and two named constables. The case was returned to the Castlebar assizes later that month,[8] where it drew special comment from Mr Justice Harrison. The bailiff and his police escort had been surrounded by 600 people, the judge noted, obliging the police to fix bayonets for their own protection. While no lives were lost, the terrified bailiff was unable to discharge his duties and, it was claimed, could not be persuaded to return to the Logboy district where, according to the RIC county inspector's report, there was 'an organized combination for resisting the law'. Anonymous letters had been received by 24 tenants threatening them with death if they paid their rents without reduction, or, in the words of the judge, if they did not 'submit to the commands of this secret and irresponsible tribunal'. The judge expressed the hope that a plentiful harvest would 'alleviate the distress from which these disturbances had originated'.[9] The degree of organization and intimidation involved in this episode of agrarian agitation strongly suggests the involvement of the secret society of Fenians, and there is some later evidence to suggest that Nolan Ferrall was targeted by Fenians.

In these circumstances, it is scarcely surprising to find that a temporary RIC station or 'hut' was established about this time at Logboy, although it was strategically positioned to also monitor the adjacent parish of Kilvine, where there was a history of agrarian trouble. Kilvine village, comprising a cluster of 95 houses, was reputed to be the 'crossest village in the province'.[10] As early as 1871 an RIC hut had been mooted for Kilvine, deemed to be 'very lawless' at that time, but the idea was dropped for want of a suitable site. Now, however, the need for a police presence in the area had become acute 'owing to the disturbed state of the neighbourhood' and Nolan Ferrall came to the rescue by providing a site.[11] An RIC officer later described the Logboy hut sub-district as the worst in the Claremorris District, being the place 'where the land agitation originated'. Nolan Ferrall's tenants, he recalled, were the very first to offer determined opposition to the service of processes.[12]

While protests on the Nolan Ferrall estate may well have been the genesis of land agitation in the locality, it was trouble on another small estate nearby that history has credited as spawning the Land League. On 20 April 1879, a Fenian-organized mass rally was held in the townland of Burris near Irishtown to demand rent reductions and, ultimately, peasant proprietorship.[13] The choice of venue has been linked to threatened evictions on the local Bourke estate although the rally's chief promoter, James Daly, claimed it was simply a convenient central location.[14] Undoubtedly it suited the tenants from several local estates, including those at Logboy and Kilvine, where agrarian disturbances had previously broken out. The fact that Burris was the scene of Famine-era mass evictions has also been suggested as a symbolic reason for its selection.[15] Coincidentally, Nolan Ferrall had been in receipt of fee-farm rent from a property at Burris which was for sale through the landed estates court in 1874.[16] This property adjoined the townland of Ballinvilla, where the Bourke's 'big house' was situated.

In any event, the Irishtown rally proved to be an unprecedented display of solidarity and resulted in the foundation of the Land League. This involved all farming classes as well as townspeople, but the clergy refused to participate. The elderly Archbishop McHale, long revered as a champion of Irish nationalism, had initially been less than enthusiastic about the Land League, urging the people to be guided by 'their faithful allies' the priests, rather than by the 'designing men' who were leading the new agitation movement. It was a sermon by Archdeacon

Kavanagh condemning those leaders that caused a second and even larger Fenian-sponsored rally to be organized a few miles away at Knock, where Kavanagh was parish priest, on 1 June.[17] On this occasion, Nolan Ferrall was singled out for public criticism, undoubtedly at the behest of the tenants on his Rockfield property nearby.[18] By the autumn, however, the clergy had been persuaded to come on board the new movement and many went on to play prominent roles, with some curates like Fr McAlpine at Ballindine and Fr Pat O'Connor at Logboy being particularly outspoken.

While Nolan Ferrall expanded his Logboy estate in 1864 by acquiring the nearby encumbered Bermingham estate, he did not avail of the opportunity to increase it further when another adjacent estate of about 100 acres at Tulrahan, formerly owned by Ferdinand Kean, came on the market in 1879. He may, of course, have simply been outbid by the eventual purchaser, one Charles Cunningham Boycott, who was soon to achieve notoriety as the eponymous target of the Land League's policy of social ostracism.[19] The more likely explanation is that Nolan Ferrall could already see that change was inevitable and that the days of landlordism in Ireland were numbered. In a letter to the *Freeman's Journal* in September, just as the Boycott affair was coming to a head, he put forward a comprehensive and carefully reasoned plan to resolve the land issue, recognizing that the pressure for peasant proprietorship had grown so strong that to deny it would cause greater evil than to concede it. His letter, running to almost 5,000 words, was in many respects a harbinger of what would eventually emerge in the Land acts. While purporting to be attractive to the landlords and the State, it also aimed to give the tenant 'the power of managing his land' and 'the right of disposing of his estate in the land'. The only restriction he would impose on tenants was an obligation in their own interest to refer disputes about boundaries, succession, etc., to independent arbitration, since otherwise 'their passion for litigation would bring many to ruin and destroy the peace of many a townland'.[20] Having presided at the petty sessions at Ballyhaunis for several years, Nolan Ferrall was well versed in the trivial issues that brought neighbours before the law, as the petty sessions' records amply testify.[21] At this time Nolan Ferrall's principal residence was at Ballybrack, Dublin; he had sub-let Logboy House and its demesne in 1879 to a wealthy London-based merchant, Thomas Barton Higson,[22] of whom nothing is known locally.

In January 1880, a correspondent for *The Times*, reporting on the widespread destitution in the vicinity of Ballyhaunis and Claremorris, warned of possible 'rebellious violence' unless prompt assistance were to be provided for the hungry.[23] Growing militancy at Logboy was evidenced by an incident that same month when shots were fired into the house of a tenant named Ronayne, narrowly missing him. The RIC believed he was targeted because he had paid his rent without securing a reduction.[24] At nearby Kilvine a serious confrontation between police and tenants occurred on 15 January when a force of 25 constables escorting a process server was attacked by a crowd estimated to be as large as

2,000.[25] After a violent struggle, some 30–40 civil bills were served.[26] The English philanthropist, James Hack Tuke, who was visiting Mayo when the 'Kilvine rioters' were later convicted, commented on the severity of the penalties meted out to them.[27]

Poverty undoubtedly contributed to this militant mood. Following a public meeting at Logboy on 25 January, a relief committee was charged with soliciting charitable funds to alleviate the 'widespread and … daily-increasing destitution'. In an obvious swipe at Nolan Ferrall, a resolution adopted at the meeting lamented the fact that there was no resident landlord to give even one day's employment. In stark contrast, another local landlord, Gerald Burke of Holywell, was 'generously and ungrudgingly' spending more than double his rental in constant employment of his own and neighbouring tenantry.[28] Already, some 200 local families were near starvation. Writing for help to the Dublin Mansion House Fund on 30 January, the local curate Fr Michael O'Donohoe said that the people were 'like wolves clamouring at my door for relief'. Crop failure and the depreciation in value of stock and produce were the main causes of their distress. Most of those in need were small farmers paying yearly rent of between £2 and £7 who had been eking out a living 'as harvest men in England', according to the parish priest, Canon Waldron. So far, the only aid received was £13 from the duchess of Marlborough's Fund. Fr O'Donohoe wrote again on 10 February to say that he had distributed meal to the 200 hungry families on the strength of a report in the *Freeman's Journal* that £50 had been granted to the committee.[29] The relief committee received further grants of £20 from the National Land League early in March,[30] and £15 from the New York Herald Relief Committee later on.[31] Two members of the Logboy committee, Luke Dillon and Thomas Delaney, both tenants of Nolan Ferrall, would soon become bitter enemies as the land war intensified; Dillon was the estate bailiff while Delaney was the chief Land League activist.

On Sunday, 21 March 1880, 'a grand demonstration' of tenant farmers took place at Logboy to set up a branch of the Irish National Land League. Well-known Fenians P.J. Gordon and John W. Nally were prominent, along with local activist Thomas Delaney.[32] In June, the new Logboy branch subscribed £3 to the Land League Relief Fund,[33] and members also attended a regional meeting in Claremorris to organize support for 100 local tenants who were threatened with eviction.[34] However, by mid-year, disillusionment was already growing in Land League ranks over the policy of peaceful parliamentary agitation.

It was always going to be difficult to sustain 'a coalition of farmers, Fenians, constitutional nationalists and shopkeepers' in pursuit of the Land League's goals. Some activists, notably James Daly, were also unhappy about the centralization of power and the minimization of local control.[35] When the first anniversary of the inaugural 1879 meeting was celebrated at Irishtown in May 1880 with C.S. Parnell and Michael Davitt present,[36] there were already grassroots rumblings of discontent about the constitutional path being pursued by the agitation leaders. The change of mood was given expression at an anti-agitation meeting at the same venue in June, chaired by a local Fenian, Daniel O'Connor, one of the organizers of the 1879 Irishtown meeting. O'Connor was now making it clear that the time for talking was over. 'Will the tongues of noisy agitators win Irish liberty?' he asked. 'No, my friends', he continued, 'other weapons will have to accompany that glorious work'. 'The rifle!' cried a voice from the crowd. Resolutions were adopted expressing dissent from the policy of parliamentary agitation, which had been 'deceptive, misleading, and inimical to the cause of Irish Nationality'.[37]

By the end of the year, it was clear that the Land League organization in the west of Ireland was being directed by Fenians.[38] Their influence was evident in the manner in which the Land League's rules were being rigorously and ruthlessly enforced. In December, a Logboy tenant named Kelly, himself a member of the Claremorris Land League committee, had to seek police protection for his cattle because 'the Logboy Land Leaguers' believed he had broken the League's rules by paying rent.[39] On Sunday 19 December, the Logboy branch announced ominously that it would hold 'an inquiry' into allegations that some members had violated the rules of the League. In a church-gate collection on the same day, the tenants raised the sum of £13 10s. for the Parnell Defence Fund.[40] Thomas Delaney forwarded it with a covering letter on behalf the people of that 'rural and rack-rented district' expressing full support for Parnell and his colleagues 'in their glorious efforts to free our land from the curse of landlordism'.[41]

The Logboy branch of the Land League, reputedly the second largest in Mayo,[42] stepped up its activities in 1881. In early January, Daniel O'Connor, whom the RIC considered to be 'a leading member of Fenian and ribbon societies and an instigator of outrage', was invited to address a public meeting at Logboy. The police were obviously there too because on 20 January O'Connor was charged with inciting the people to forcibly dispossess the holders of 'certain farms in or near Irishtown'.[43] Soon afterwards, for using inflammatory language at Logboy, he was interned in Kilmainham gaol until December under the recently-enacted Protection of Person and Property Act.[44] The following month, his fellow Fenian, P.J. Gordon, was also jailed for 12 months for inciting to murder. In May, the secretary of the Logboy branch, Patrick Crawley, attended a meeting of the National Land League in Dublin,[45] and he was back there again in September for the National Convention, chaired by Parnell, to consider the new Land act.[46]

Logboy was one of the first places in the country to form a branch of the Ladies Land League, pledging itself to cooperate with Anna Parnell 'in her untiring efforts to carry on the agitation until justice is granted to us'. This happened on 30 January 1881,[47] just a few days after Davitt had first proposed the idea of a women's organization, headed by Parnell's sister, to step in should arrests cripple the existing League.[48] Anna Parnell herself visited the locality the next month and she was warmly welcomed at Ballyhaunis on 14 February by Logboy curate, Fr Michael O'Donohoe.[49]

6 'An eviction scene in the west of Ireland, 1881' (*Illustrated London News*, 19 March 1881)

The Land League's policy of enforcing rent reductions soon led to the threat of evictions. In the House of Commons on 24 March, T.P. O'Connor MP asked whether 70 ejectments had been served on the tenants of Nolan Ferrall.[50] One of these threatened evictions was highlighted at a meeting of the National Ladies' Land League in Dublin on 19 April, the tenant concerned being a blind man who was paying rent of £3 4s. 6d. on a holding valued at £1 17s. 6d.[51]

Matters eventually came to a head on 14 August when 11 evictions were carried out for non-payment of rent. The Logboy Land League took care of the most destitute of the evicted while the others were readmitted as caretakers.[52] The press reported a particularly distressing scene when the sheriff's bailiffs removed a man named Flatley 'from his death bed' and left him outside on a litter of straw.[53] This type of image had been brought to the attention of the English public by Aloysius O'Kelly's sketch of an eviction scene in the west of Ireland published a few months earlier (fig. 6).[54] The report brought a swift riposte from the landlord. Writing on 20 August from Wiesbaden, a spa town in Germany, Nolan Ferrall pointed out that the evictions were a mere technicality to secure legal possession and that the tenants in questions had immediately been allowed back into their houses as caretakers. He denied any harsh treatment of Flatley, claiming that the man's two well-off sons had refused to help with their father's arrears. The inference was clear: those who could well afford to pay were simply refusing to do so, under Land League pressure. Whatever the manner of his treatment, the unfortunate Flatley was dead three weeks later.[55] Feelings were now running high on the estate.

On the morning of Friday, 18 November 1881, the body of Luke Dillon, the 52-year-old estate bailiff for Nolan Ferrall, was discovered on the roadside near his home at Logboy with gunshot wounds to the head and chest.[56] The RIC quickly classified his killing as an agrarian crime, motivated by ill-feeling on the part of tenants who blamed him for the landlord's refusal to grant them rent reductions. The police also knew that there was bad blood between Dillon and Thomas Delaney, treasurer of the Logboy branch of the Land League.[57] Dillon seemed to have been well-liked and respected, evidenced by the large attendance at his funeral.[58] He was said to have been 'on the best of terms with his neighbours', even on occasion lending money to tenants in need. There was 'not a more popular man in that part of the country', a former Land League officer later told the Special Commission (*The Times* v Parnell),[59] prompting Counsel for *The Times* to quip: 'Was it on account of his excessive popularity that he was murdered?'[60] This benign view of Dillon, who had been bailiff since about 1865,[61] was not universally shared, however. Folklore recorded in the US by a descendant of Logboy emigrants recalled Dillon's role in 'evicting and burning the cottages of those tenants that could not pay rent' and in preventing access to the water pump on the estate, forcing tenants to walk a mile to the nearest well.[62] There were suspicions that his murderers had local knowledge because the crime was committed when the local RIC were preoccupied elsewhere.[63] Mrs Dillon herself had no doubt as to the identity of the culprits, publicly announcing that they were actually present in her house on the night of her husband's wake.[64]

It is simplistic to assume that Land League politicization was behind all rural violence and intimidation of this period.[65] Personal feuds were often played out under the convenient banner of politics, as has been highlighted in a Co. Kerry study.[66] In Luke Dillon's case, it is difficult to disentangle personal animosities from those linked to his role as bailiff. Some locals, including the parish priest,[67] believed that robbery was the probable motive for his murder.[68] Mrs Dillon, in her compensation claim, confirmed that her husband had been robbed of about £25, equivalent to half his annual income from the job, but she was convinced that the robbery was opportunistic and that the real motive had to do with her husband's role as bailiff. The RIC clearly suspected Land League involvement, knowing that Dillon was blamed for the landlord's refusal to grant a rent reduction. Their suspicions fell on Thomas Delaney, given his bad relations with Dillon. But there was also a rumour circulating that one of their own members was implicated in the crime. Years later the bailiff's son would be cross-examined about this rumour at the Special Commission in London. He was asked by Sir Charles Russell (counsel for Parnell) whether he knew anything about a Logboy-based policeman being charged with his father's murder and then being transferred and dismissed, but that line of questioning was dropped abruptly following an objection by the other side.[69] Intriguingly, a Roscommon-born policeman named John Turbett who was stationed at Logboy in 1881 was indeed transferred from Mayo in June 1882 and was dismissed from the force later that month although the circumstances are not recorded;[70] in August he was charged with threatening to kill the RIC Inspector-General but was acquitted on grounds of insanity,[71] and detained in Richmond Lunatic Asylum.[72]

Thomas Delaney, the local Land League activist, was the landlord's nemesis. This emerges clearly from Nolan Ferrall's correspondence with the Dublin authorities in March–April 1882, which also sheds light on the events leading up to the bailiff's murder. Writing to the RIC Inspector General from Bray on 29 March 1882, Nolan Ferrall was scathing about Delaney's role as *agent provocateur* in the locality: 'The chief agitator ... is Thomas Delaney ... with whose character and acts and crimes you are, I believe, well acquainted'. Delaney, he said, had 'powerful support in his lawlessness in his brother-in-law, the Catholic curate, a most violent firebrand whose language in Logboy Catholic church last November a few days before the murder of my bailiff Luke Dillon was then, I believe, reported to you as having led to the murder'.[73] One wonders whether Nolan Ferrall may even have complained to the curate's superiors about his behaviour because it seems more than a coincidence that Fr O'Connor, who had only come to Logboy in 1881, should find himself transferred to Achill Island the following year by the new archbishop, John McEvilly.[74] McEvilly's political views were very different to those of his predecessor McHale, although he avoided publicizing his opposition to the Fenians and the Land League.[75] Priests whom he believed to have been overly tolerated by McHale soon came under his scrutiny, however, and those showing any inclination for political engagement quickly found themselves on the move.[76] If Fr O'Connor's transfer was indeed designed to curb his outspokenness, it certainly did not have the desired effect. He was as forthright as ever in 1894, when he welcomed the Land League's founder, Michael Davitt, to Achill with the words: 'When famine swept over this island, and the callous government of England looked carelessly on, you came promptly to our aid'.[77]

Nolan Ferrall clearly wanted rid of Delaney at all costs. An opportunity presented itself when Delaney, having fallen into arrears of rent, was forced to sell back his interest in two farms to the landlord at a sheriff's sale, which was a more frequent occurrence during the Land War than were agrarian crimes or evictions.[78] The removal of Delaney, Nolan Ferrall reasoned, would send the right signal to the rest of the tenants and peace would be restored. With Delaney out of the way, the landlord proposed to hand over his vacated house, a substantial slated structure, for conversion into a permanent police barracks. The local RIC officer, in supporting Nolan Ferrall's proposal, remarked that 'Delaney is the cause of the bad feeling still existing between Mr Ferrall and his Logboy tenantry'. However, his superiors were less enamoured of the proposal.[79]

Having failed to persuade the RIC of its merits, Nolan Ferrall raised his barracks proposal directly with the chief secretary, W.E. Forster, in a letter on 22 April 1882.[80] He reminded Forster of their conversation shortly after the Dillon inquest at the end of 1881 when he had actually named the suspected accomplices in the bailiff's murder as Thomas Delaney, the Land League activist, and Michael Murphy. In later visits to Mayo he had gained oral corroboration of their involvement, he said, most recently on 17 April when an unnamed local had given him 'a circumstantial account of the murder'. He also reminded the chief secretary of the role of Delaney's brother-in-law, Fr O'Connor, who had denounced bailiffs and landlords from the pulpit of Logboy church on the Sunday before Dillon's murder. Nolan Ferrall also took the opportunity to explain how, a year earlier, he had been obliged to get ejectment decrees against some 15 tenants for non-payment of rent. In the meantime, however, he had offered to take all of them back 'on very easy terms' and while most, if not all, were agreeable to this, they were afraid of Delaney and dared not accept 'for fear of being visited at night and murdered'.

Nolan Ferrall's plans were to be frustrated, however. In a further letter to the authorities on 28 April, he regretted that he was now obliged to withdraw his barracks proposal because of a title problem with Delaney's house. He still expressed the hope that Delaney could be arrested under the Protection of Person and Property Act for complicity in Dillon's murder. Delaney's removal would, he argued, be 'generally felt as a welcome relief from terrorism'.[81] The RIC, however, demurred. On the contrary, they believed that Delaney's arrest 'would have the effect of making people in the neighbourhood who are beginning to talk more freely on the matter, more reticent than ever'.[82] Besides, the rent control measures introduced by the Land Act of 1881 had already taken the sting out of the land agitation movement.

In 1881 the population of the Logboy estate was little more than half of what it had been four decades earlier. Death and emigration in times of distress had taken a severe toll. Yet, for most of the quarter century since Nolan Ferrall had acquired the estate, relations between him and his tenants appeared to have been civil, if not cordial. However, the 'perfect storm' of misfortunes that arose in the late 1870s set the scene for a showdown between landlord and tenant at Logboy. By 1878 there was a concerted campaign against paying rent with some tenants even receiving death threats for failure to cooperate. The resulting threat of evictions led to the attacks on the process server in 1879. The large numbers involved in those incidents demonstrated that there was considerable external support for the tenants. By then, Nolan Ferrall himself had recognized that change was inevitable, even if he abhorred the 'mischievous influences' promoting it, and he formulated detailed proposals for managing that change in a peaceful manner that, he felt, would satisfy the demands of all interested parties: landlords, tenants and the state. However, the years 1879 to 1881 were marked by intensive Land League activity at Logboy and in the adjacent parish of Kilvine orchestrated by outside activists that led to confrontation and evictions and culminated in the murder of the estate bailiff.

The mystery of the murder of the bailiff, Luke Dillon, was never solved. It emerged from testimony given to the Special Commission that Dillon had received a death threat shortly before his murder. The text of the threatening letter, discovered after Dillon's death, was read into the record by *The Times'* Counsel. It stated that 120 men were present when it was written and that each was sworn to shoot Dillon.[83] Even allowing for hyperbole, this does suggest that at least some locals had knowledge of the intimidation of Dillon. Nevertheless, despite the inducement of a £300 reward for information leading to a conviction, nobody came forward and the police investigation proved fruitless.[84]

Nolan Ferrall's decision to finally abandon Logboy in the wake of his bailiff's murder must have been difficult for him given the family's long association with Logboy and the west of Ireland. In his 'peasant proprietary' proposal, he had referred to a landlord's attachment to his hereditary land as being 'a natural and honourable sentiment'. His proposal to reserve the sporting and certain other rights to the landlord would, he felt, be sufficient to induce landlords to surrender their beneficial ownership while continuing to reside on their estates, thus maintaining 'a connection with the occupiers and an interest in their welfare, instead of severing classes wholly'. It was a solution that he hoped 'would remove all conflicts of interests without destroying the ties of sympathy and good will'. What emerged in Gladstone's Land Act of 1881 was not quite what Nolan Ferrall had envisaged. As a mechanism for transferring landownership from landlord to tenant, the Act was a failure, with only 700 tenants overall opting to purchase.[85] However, by conceding the 'three Fs' (fair rent, free sale and fixity of tenure), the Act took the heat out of land agitation, although it is not surprising that fissures in the agitation movement were already appearing since alliances crossing social boundaries are seldom enduring.[86] Landlords, meanwhile, were less than happy with the Act, as will be seen in the next chapter.

4. End-game: 'a peasant proprietary'

The real significance of the 1881 Land Act lay in its operation as 'a device for controlling rent' by means of new land courts empowered to determine fair rents.[1] In the first wave of rent revisions these courts had granted reductions of 20 per cent on average,[2] and eligible tenants understandably had rushed to avail of this exceptional deal. However, the tenants most in need of relief, namely those who were in arrears, did not qualify, which meant that nearly two-thirds of Mayo tenants were excluded.[3] This anomaly was quickly rectified by the Arrears Act of 1882, an outcome of the Kilmainham Treaty between Gladstone and Parnell, which enabled the Land Commission to cancel arrears of £30 or less. With these concessions secured, Parnell in effect called off the Land War.[4]

While these concessions may well have blunted anti-landlordism,[5] landlords themselves were less than happy about the *quid pro quo*, the usurping of their traditional property rights. The extinction of rent arrears was particularly galling.[6] Nolan Ferrall was quick to highlight this injustice in a letter to *The Times* in May 1882 claiming it would deprive landlords of at least half a year's income – and up to three years' income in many cases. Meanwhile, he pointed out, the landlords' own financial commitments remained unchanged. They still had to meet onerous mortgage repayments while the state would continue 'to levy income-tax, quit-rent, and tithe-rent-charge on the very income which it has confiscated.' The remedy he proposed 'for this and other sufferings inflicted on Irish landowners by the recent land legislation' was simple and cost-free: the state should provide loans at 3 per cent, redeemable at 3½ per cent, to enable landowners to pay off all mortgages. The state would probably gain rather than lose in this exercise, he argued.[7] In November, Nolan Ferrall himself was appointed an investigator under the Arrears Act.[8]

After 1882, an uneasy peace may have reigned for a while but the events of the Land War were not quickly forgotten, rather they 'created lasting bitterness in the Big House'.[9] At Logboy, relations between Nolan Ferrall and his tenants had inevitably been soured by the unsolved murder of his estate bailiff and by his frustrating failure to have the chief local agitator removed. He must also have been unnerved by the unsolved murder in June 1882 of his fellow-landlord, Walter M. Bourke,[10] who lived at Curraghleagh House not far from his own Rockfield property. By 1883 Nolan Ferrall had effectively abandoned Logboy House for his own safety. In August of that year he was based at Bray, Co. Wicklow, when he took legal action against a Logboy tenant, Patrick Finnegan, for refusing to vacate a house at Ballynastockagh.[11] Soon afterwards he moved

7 'Outside the land court at Claremorris, 1881' (*Illustrated London News*, 26 Nov. 1881)

into Dublin; he was residing at 2 Palmerston Villas, Rathmines, when he contributed to a renovation fund for Rathgar church.[12] In 1884, he was ranked at 90 in the top 100 ratepayers in Co. Mayo and he was one of only 22 classed as non-resident.[13]

It was not just the Logboy tenants that were making life difficult for Nolan Ferrall. The tenants on his Rockfield property near Knock were also proving recalcitrant, refusing to pay rent unless they got an abatement. Three years earlier, through his agent Edwin Thomas, he had granted these tenants a reduction of 10 per cent while those who had paid a full year's rent received a 25 per cent reduction.[14] This time, however, he instituted eviction proceedings against 11 families who were in default and in September 1883 the evictions were duly executed, although all bar one were allowed to return to their houses as caretakers.[15]

Among the many who had moved quickly to seek judicial rent reviews in the local land court at Claremorris (fig. 7) were several of Nolan Ferrall's tenants at Logboy, who managed to secure reductions averaging 21 per cent. However, in most cases the decision was appealed, generally by the landlord although a small number of tenants also appealed. These appeals, 22 in all, were considered by the Land Commission court of appeal sitting in Castlebar in early November 1883. The landlord's solicitor claimed that the recent murder of the bailiff had prevented him from defending his rent levels before the initial hearing. Eight of the appeals were withdrawn when called. Of the remainder, the appeal court confirmed the judicial rent in six cases but raised it in seven, of which four were 'by consent'.[16]

The tenants were represented by P.J.B. Daly, the Ballinrobe solicitor who defended many tenants and agitators during the course of the Land War and who had signed Parnell's nomination papers as a candidate for Mayo in the 1880 general election. Ironically, Daly, himself a landlord, would soon become a target of land agitation, jointly with Nolan Ferrall.

Meanwhile, Nolan Ferrall hadn't neglected the family of his murdered bailiff. On 6 August 1884, he called personally to the Chief Secretary's Office in Dublin Castle with a view to expediting payment of the £500 compensation due to Mrs Dillon under the Prevention of Crime (Ireland) Act, 1882.[17] Her son, John Dillon, who had succeeded his late father as bailiff, had gone to live on the Rockfield property but continued to act as bailiff over Logboy. He was a witness for the landlord when the latter sued a Logboy tenant, Mary Conway of Lurgan, for trespass and refusing to vacate a house.[18] She was later awarded a grant of £1 by the Irish National League, which had succeeded the Land League.[19] It may be indicative of the landlord's waning interest in the Logboy community that the local church, the construction of which his uncle had sponsored over four decades earlier, had fallen into a very dilapidated state by 1885.[20]

By 1886, the land issue was firmly back on the nationalist agenda because of the on-going agricultural recession. Although the land courts had reduced rents considerably since 1881, this concession had been more than offset by the 30 per cent drop in the general Irish agricultural price over the same period. A groundswell of agrarian unrest was developing again. When Nolan Ferrall's agent, Edwin Thomas, held a rent collection office in Ballyhaunis in late November, the Logboy tenants demanded an abatement of between 30 and 40 per cent and when this was rejected, they refused to pay anything, instead lodging the withheld amounts with the trustees of a 'No Rent' fund. At the same time, the tenants on the nearby More O'Farrell estate had accepted an offer of a 24 per cent rent reduction and all of them paid up, their arrears having been discharged by payment of one year's rent.[21]

The growing unrest was demonstrated at a rally at Irishtown on the last Sunday of December, attended by an estimated 10,000 farmers from counties Mayo, Galway and Roscommon. The Claremorris activist, P.J. Gordon, expressed delight at seeing such a vast multitude assembled 'in the old spot where the Land League cradle got its first rock'. He threatened Nolan Ferrall with 'another new weapon called the Plan of Campaign',[22] a strategy first outlined by John Dillon MP at a meeting in support of Lord Clanricarde's tenants at Woodford, Co. Galway, the previous October.[23] It was essentially a device for collective bargaining on individual estates,[24] whereby a group of tenants would offer what they considered to be a fair rent and if the landlord refused to compromise, the proffered rent would be withheld and paid into an escrow account managed by trustees pending a settlement.[25] This fund was also used to support evicted tenants. The adoption of the Plan of Campaign signalled the start of a second phase of land war, targeting at least 20 estates in Co. Mayo in the years 1887–8.[26]

Pressure on Nolan Ferrall was intensified at a public meeting in Claremorris on 19 January 1887, when John Redmond MP hailed the success of the Plan of Campaign in bringing Lord Dillon to his senses and forcing him to reach a compromise with his tenants. Redmond believed that this victory could be replicated on the Nolan Ferrall estate. Daniel Crilly MP said the aim of the Plan was to put down unjust landlordism. If Nolan Farrell had any common sense, he said, he would follow the example of Lord Dillon: 'I tell Nolan Farrell from this platform today, that should I go to prison, or should Mr Redmond go to prison, he has yet to deal with the tenants on his estate, and so long as they are willing to pay him what is justly due to him, so long as he refuses to accept that, you shall have the support of the English and Scotch people'. Calling for the reinstatement of those tenants recently evicted from the Nolan Ferrall estate, he promised that, in the meantime, they would be well looked after by the organizers of the Plan.[27]

P.J. Gordon was characteristically forthright in his appeal to 'the men of Logboy', praising those who had adhered to the Plan but castigating a small minority who had secretly paid up despite publicly proclaiming support for the Plan.[28] The prime targets of the Plan were the economically vulnerable landlords,[29] and clearly Nolan Ferrall was seen as one of those. Gordon, obviously well informed, stated that Nolan Ferrall had mortgaged his property for £20,000 and having squandered all the money, had emigrated and now wanted more money 'in order to support the landlords in a foreign country'. Gordon said he had visited the Logboy estate and found appalling conditions there, worse than on any other estate in Co. Mayo: 'I can say here today that the cabins occupied by the cow or the ass on other properties are superior to the cabins occupied by the people on the Nolan Ferrall property'. He announced that 'there will be a meeting in that historic spot, Irishtown, next Sunday, and if I have life in me I shall be there'.[30]

The Irishtown meeting duly took place on Sunday, 23 January, and a large contingent from Logboy attended.[31] It was now abundantly clear that serious trouble was brewing. Just a few days earlier a summons-server named Daly en route to the Nolan Ferrall estate had been attacked and pelted with stones and mud by locals who believed that he was intent on serving ejectment notices. Daly had drawn a revolver and threatened to fire, but had to run for his life.[32] The following month Logboy was the scene of a major confrontation between tenants and state authorities. Having adopted the Plan of Campaign, all but four of the tenants had been served with processes of ejectment. The four in question, who were somewhat better off than their neighbours, were served with writs for the amounts of rent due.[33] Determined resistance to the enforcement of these writs was obviously anticipated since a large force of police was drafted into Ballyhaunis on the night of Thursday, 24 February, to assist in this task.[34] The Ballyhaunis townspeople refused to provide the police with transport to Logboy despite threats that those publicans who failed to cooperate would have their licences withdrawn.

Nevertheless on the following morning the sheriff's bailiff, accompanied by about 250 police under Resident Magistrate Cecil Roche, proceeded to the house of James Murray, one of the four tenants, at Derryhog. Word had quickly spread that the police and bailiffs were coming and a crowd of about 2,000 had assembled on the Murray farm prior to their arrival.[35] Access to the house, by means of a bridge spanning a small river surrounding the farm, was blocked by the crowd but the police placed pontoon bridges across the river without opposition. However, violence broke out after a section of the police baton-charged a group of jeering children, who took refuge in the crowd. The crowd responded with a volley of stones. The police had been ordered to about-face and prepare to fire when Canon Waldron intervened and further violence was averted.[36] This episode is still recalled in local folklore as 'the eviction at Derryhog that never happened'.[37]

On the following Sunday, 27 February, an estimated 12,000 people assembled in the grounds of Logboy House to protest against the threatened evictions, both on the Nolan Ferrall estate and on the Irishtown estate of P.J.B. Daly, the solicitor who had earlier represented the Logboy tenants.[38] Nolan Ferrall's residence, now vacant, was commandeered to provide a platform for speakers. On this occasion, the police were conspicuous by their absence, 'the promoters having stolen a march on the authorities'.[39] A local newspaper published the names of 48 people who were present. The meeting adopted three resolutions. The first reaffirmed allegiance to the National cause until Ireland had the right of making her own laws. The second congratulated John Dillon, William O'Brien, Daniel Crilly and the other traversers on the defeat they inflicted on the government in the recent state trials. The Irish National League branches at Logboy and Bekan had contributed to a defence fund in aid of those prosecuted in the trials,[40] and one of the defendants, Daniel Crilly MP, addressed the meeting and received a great ovation. The third resolution promised to carry the Plan of Campaign to a successful conclusion in the locality.

The momentum was maintained with a further 'immense meeting' at Logboy in April to protest against coercion. A resolution against land-grabbing was passed, reaffirming the people's determination 'never to cease constitutional agitation till the props of tyrannical landlords are put down'. Once again, the indefatigable P.J. Gordon addressed the meeting, condemning land-grabbing and exhorting the people to stick to the Plan of Campaign and 'the teachings of the National League'.[41] In May, another fruitless attempt was made to make a seizure at the Murray holding.[42] It wasn't until December, after many of his fellow landlords had already conceded, that Nolan Ferrall finally relented and granted his tenants a reduction of 25 per cent on all rent and arrears due, thus bringing the protracted dispute to an end.[43]

For the most part, the following decade appears to have been relatively trouble-free at Logboy. There was still some nationalist activity. The local branch of the Irish National League contributed to the Blunt Defence Fund in 1888 in aid of Wilfred Scawen Blunt, the English poet and writer who spent two months in Kilmainham jail for participating in a proscribed meeting at Woodford in support of the Clanricarde tenants.[44] Logboy Nationalists presented an address to Parnell when he came to a meeting in Irishtown on Sunday, 19 April 1891.[45] Meanwhile, the threat of endemic starvation may have receded but there were still occasional food shortages. In 1890, for example, about half of the potato crop was lost in the Electoral Division of Culnacleha in which Logboy was situated.[46] In 1894, in a major parish reorganization, the Logboy townlands were transferred from Annagh parish to Bekan, but this administrative change probably had little impact since the Logboy faithful retained their own church and curate.

The landlord was again involved in litigation during this period. The case of Nolan Ferrall v Curran and others was listed for hearing before the queen's bench, chancery division of the high court on 26 July 1890.[47] Two-and-a-half years later, the landlord appears in the law lists again when 'J.N. Ferrall' is one of the cases listed for hearing before Mr Justice Monroe (land judge) in the chancery division of the high court on 11 January 1893.[48] The outcome appears to have been that the estate was once more in receivership, since the following year it was Messrs Kendal & Hazel, 'the newly-appointed receivers', who held the rent collection office in Ballyhaunis. On this occasion every tenant paid a half-year's rent but that did not satisfy the receivers who threatened legal proceedings to recover arrears. The tenants indicated their intention of petitioning the chief receiver and, if necessary, the chancery judge to secure a reasonable rent reduction having regard to 'the depressed condition of the country'. At the same time it was reported that three eviction notices from this estate had been served on the Claremorris board of guardians.[49]

In April 1895, some four decades after he had purchased the Logboy property, John Nolan Ferrall died at his home in Dublin, at the age of 63. He was buried in the family plot in Glasnevin cemetery. His demise brought down the curtain on the family's centuries-long relationship with Logboy. The death of the landlord did not, of course, signal an end to the tenants' concerns. Two years on, rent payments were still an issue when, in October 1897, tenants on the Lurgan part of the estate were refusing to pay until granted substantial reductions.[50] The following year a third phase of the Land War began when William O'Brien launched a new political movement, the United Irish League, at Westport in January 1898. Building on the success of the Plan of Campaign, in which O'Brien had been a key figure, its main objective was through popular agitation to force the government to buy out the large 'ranches' and redistribute them among the small tenant farmers. By 1901 membership of the League had grown to over 1,150 branches countrywide with over 120,000 members,[51] and ultimately it developed into the official organization of the Irish Parliamentary Party. To promote the new organization in east Mayo, John O'Donnell of Westport, O'Brien's protégé and later MP for South Mayo, visited Bekan, Aghamore and Ballyhaunis in February 1898.[52] His publicity campaign was boosted by a mass meeting at Knock on Sunday, 25 May 1898, which was addressed by O'Brien and Michael Davitt

MP. The attendance included a large group of tenants from Bekan parish, of which Logboy now formed part. It was a time of severe distress in the locality. People were facing a famine that had no parallel 'since the disastrous years of '47 and '49', according to the parish priest of Knock.[53] A branch of the United Irish League was formed at Logboy in early November,[54] inspired no doubt by the League's rally at Irishtown on Sunday, 23 October 1898, which was addressed by Davitt and attended by a large group of Logboy tenants.[55]

The next three years were relatively uneventful at Logboy but in December 1901 the tenants collectively met the receiver, Mr Hazel, in Ballyhaunis concerning their demand for a rent reduction of 21 per cent. It was not forthcoming so they withheld all rent pending a concession and meanwhile, in line with the Plan of Campaign strategy, they deposited the rent money in a special fund.[56] At an after-Mass meeting in Logboy on Sunday, 12 January 1902, the president of the branch, Michael Cleary, promised to get the Nolan Ferrall tenants 'into fighting trim'. They had all joined the Tenants' Defence Association, which had been founded in October 1889 in response to the formation of a landlords' syndicate to resist the Plan of Campaign,[57] and which had infused new life into the agrarian agitation.[58] They were pledged to fight 'to the bitter end' to get a rent reduction and Frank Burke, Secretary of the South Mayo Executive of the UIL, saw no reason why they shouldn't achieve a 30 per cent reduction like the Congested Districts' Board had given the former Dillon tenants.[59] A few weeks later, Cleary gave an update to the branch members on their financial position. The 'war chest', he said, was increasing daily and they were getting support from tenants on other estates. Special tribute was paid to the traders and merchants of Ballyhaunis who had contributed over £25 to the Logboy fund despite also having recently subscribed to the De Freyne estate fund.[60]

Meanwhile, the branch wrote to the UIL Standing Committee in Dublin seeking financial support in the event of their cattle being seized for non-payment of rent, as otherwise the tenants were likely to settle. They received a non-committal reply from Laurence Ginnell saying that the tenants on the other local estates in dispute, namely Murphy and De Freyne, had not asked the Committee to assume any responsibility.[61] Simultaneously, Ginnell raised their request with John Redmond MP saying that the Committee was reluctant to categorically reject it outright lest publication of the refusal 'would be injurious to the tenants on all other associated estates'.[62]

In April, decrees were issued against those Logboy tenants on the Nolan Ferrall estate who were holding out for rent reductions on a par with the Dillon tenants. In June there was another botched attempt by the sheriff's officer, accompanied by bailiff John Dillon and a force of police, to make seizures on various Logboy farms. At the same time, a 'combination' of tenants on the Nolan Ferrall property at Rockfield was also pressing for a rent reduction in line with the Dillon tenants.[63] The next month, the Logboy tenants repeated their refusal to pay any rent without an abatement, a demand that the receiver, Hazel, rejected out of hand. Meanwhile, the Rockfield tenants, in solidarity, refused to pay until a final settlement was made with their fellow tenants at Logboy.[64]

Over the next 18 months, the Logboy tenants saw considerable progress being made towards realizing their dreams of becoming owner occupiers. In December 1902, the chief secretary for Ireland, George Wyndham, backed a new scheme for tenant land purchase worked out at a landlord-tenant conference. The Logboy branch of the United Irish League had conveyed their views on the scheme in correspondence with William O'Brien MP in April 1903.[65] The resulting Wyndham Land Purchase Act of 1903 signalled the end of landlordism in Ireland and ushered in a new era of agrarian peace.[66] The following year, through the good offices of Archdeacon Kilkenny PP, Claremorris, negotiations for the purchase of the Nolan Ferrall estate were successfully completed,[67] although a delay of some years would intervene before the estate would definitively transfer to the tenants.[68]

By the dawn of the 20th century, material conditions in rural Ireland were improving and modest signs of renewed confidence and community spirit were emerging at Logboy. In 1900, the Logboy Agricultural Society was founded and the following year it had 21 members and had issued 13 loans.[69] In 1903, a new school was opened, replacing the building that the Logboy landlord had been instrumental in procuring some six decades before.[70] Once the Congested Districts' Board purchased the Nolan Ferrall estate, the Logboy tenants could at last consider themselves to be masters of their own destiny. Perhaps the most powerful symbol of the end of landlordism in the area was the demolition of Logboy House and the recycling of the building materials to construct new cottages for some of the tenants. It remained to be seen whether the new owners would fare better as landowners than they had as tenants. Would 'the magic of property turn sand into gold'?[71]

Conclusion

The history of 19th-century Ireland is, in many respects, the history of the landed estates, yet the study of individual estates has been largely neglected or ignored by historians. The few studies that have been done generally concern the larger estates and, as Curtis cautioned, 'it is risky to draw even mildly dogmatic conclusions about Irish landlords as a whole from the anatomy of one or two estates, no matter what their size and resources'.[1] The present study demonstrates the potential that exists for fruitful research at estate level, even where the estate is relatively small and obscure, and even in the absence of a ready-made body of source material, in particular estate papers.

At first glance, the Nolan Ferrall estate holds little attraction for the historian. It seemed scarcely to have registered on history's Richter scale or, if it had, little evidence of that has survived. There was no rich vein of source material waiting to be mined, no colourful folklore about famine, evictions, or rack-renting landlords. The former custodians of the Logboy estate were 'kindly remembered and as landlords went, they were not hard' according to a local verdict from around 1940,[2] which echoed sentiments expressed in the folklore collected by local schoolchildren in the late 1930s.[3] Even the murder of the estate bailiff, which must have convulsed the community in 1881, had been largely erased from folk memory. The only tangible reminders of the landlord's presence were the church, segments of the demesne wall and some exotic trees. Yet by delving into a wide range of primary sources it has been possible to trace, in broad outline at least, the evolution of the estate over seven decades of turbulent Irish history and to reveal some surprising discoveries.

Irish landlords have long had a bad press, although their tarnished image has been somewhat rehabilitated in recent decades. One of the aims of this study was to ascertain where the Logboy landlords fitted on the scale between 'bad' and 'good', between 'rack-renter' and 'recklessly generous'. The first of the two landlords considered in the study, Edmond Nolan, was placed in a rather difficult position on inheriting Logboy. He was already established in the legal profession in Dublin. His remote country estate was in debt, yet he could neither dispose of it nor generate extra rental income given the economic recession. Fortunately, because he had independent means, he could treat the Logboy estate as a status symbol, a country retreat for leisure activities such as hunting and shooting. He exhibited many of the traits of a paternalistic landlord of the time, being instrumental in providing a new school and church and supplying food aid to his tenants in times of shortage. Like landlords generally, he had little incentive to try to control the subdivision of holdings that facilitated an unsustainable growth of the estate population, part of a national problem that would ultimately lead to Malthusian catastrophe.

The second landlord, John Nolan Ferrall, was also independently wealthy. Having inherited part of the extensive Ferrall estates in Co. Roscommon, he proceeded to amass an impressive property portfolio, snapping up several more indebted estates, like the Logboy estate, that came on the market through the encumbered estates court in the 1850s. Credit was readily available; he borrowed £25,000 from a London insurance company to fund one property transaction. This expansion was matched by his possession in the 1860s of all the trappings of success – a stylish townhouse in Dublin, a luxury yacht for Mediterranean cruises, a well-stocked hunting/fishing lodge in scenic Mayo. This lifestyle, however, would be short-lived; the yacht had already gone by 1867 and more asset-stripping would soon follow.

The study demonstrates that both landlord and tenant alike were, in large measure, victims of circumstance. Their fortunes were inextricably linked, making it 'virtually impossible for either party to escape unscathed from the misfortunes of the other'.[4] The difference, of course, was that those misfortunes might be a matter of life and death for the tenant whereas they rarely had such serious repercussions for the landlord. The study establishes that on two occasions the Logboy estate ran into deep financial difficulties and ended up in receivership. The Great Famine precipitated the first crisis, the Land War the second. Despite the dearth of direct evidence about the Logboy tenants at the time of the Famine, the decimation of the population during that decade and the horror stories of death and starvation from the immediate locality strongly support the view that the tenants were not spared a harrowing experience.

The post-Famine economic recovery did not spell the end of the tenants' troubles. By 1881, death and emigration had reduced the estate population to half the 1841 level. The second financial crisis arose during the Land War. Although rents generally had remained moderate for decades, barely doubling between 1815 and 1875, the land courts of 1881 delivered cuts averaging around 20 per cent for the tenants and thereafter further concessions were extracted through pressure exerted by the Plan of Campaign and the United Irish League. Not surprisingly, the Logboy estate was again in receivership when John Nolan Ferrall died in 1895.

Perhaps the most unexpected research discovery was that, despite almost three decades of apparent tranquillity after the Famine, the Logboy estate should be at the heart of the agrarian agitation that spawned the Land League, and that it remained a trouble spot during the second and third phases of the Land War. While Edmond Nolan's pre-Famine tenure was characteristic of the 'moral economy' of that era, with deferential tenants and a paternalistic landlord, there was a 'steady erosion of deference' as the century wore on,[5] and the 'traditional hierarchies and mutualities in rural society' came to be challenged.[6] When the crisis of the late 1870s arose, the world was a very different place. The tenants were no longer afraid or unwilling to challenge the establishment, whether landlord, state or church. Moreover, their ability to organize and their openness to outside influences were facilitated by the dramatic improvement in communications brought about by increased literacy, diversity of newspapers, enhanced mail service, and the advent of the railway and the telegraph.

Thus, when the poverty crisis arose around 1877–8, the Logboy tenants were in no mood to accept it fatalistically and were also better placed to organize and link up with outside activists. They quickly came together to arrange relief and solicit charitable funds. Most significantly, they were among the very first Mayo tenants to engage in concerted action, undoubtedly instigated by Fenian activists, to demand rent reductions and to violently resist threatened evictions. This action included a campaign of intimidation against some tenants and attacks on a process-server and his police escort in 1879. The authorities responded by establishing a temporary RIC station at Logboy to deal with the growing 'lawlessness' in that locality and in the adjacent Kilvine parish, scene of the famous Irishtown rally on 20 April 1879.

Nolan Ferrall was realistic enough to recognize that change was coming and he even drew up detailed proposals for the government as to how a 'peasant proprietary' might be achieved in a manner that would satisfy landlords, tenants and the state alike. Nevertheless, given the family's centuries-long association with Logboy, the idea of relinquishing the estate must have been difficult for him to accept. In his proposal, he had argued that if a landlord were allowed retain the sporting and certain other rights over the estate, he would have an incentive to stay in residence and maintain an interest in the welfare of the tenants. However, the campaign to abolish landlordism grew ever stronger and the idea of a landlord remaining on to live in harmony with his former tenants was only a pipe dream. Nolan Ferrall was targeted by the Plan of Campaign in 1887 when two decisive events occurred at Logboy, reflecting the growing self-confidence of the tenants. First, a crowd of 2,000 protestors faced down a police-backed attempt to enforce a writ. Second, the estate itself was chosen as the venue for a mass rally against threated evictions and the abandoned Logboy House was occupied. Eventually, after his fellow landlords had relented, Nolan Ferrall too conceded a rent reduction. After his death, there was a final round of agitation around the turn of the century under the flag of the United Irish League.

The break-up of the Nolan Ferrall estate marked the end of a landlord-tenant regime at Logboy that spanned some two-and-a-half centuries. This study has sought to gain a better understanding of the evolution of the Logboy estate community, landlord and tenant alike, during the seven decades of frequent turmoil leading up to that defining landmark. The main significance of the study lies in the fact that it charts the experiences on a small, Catholic-owned estate in this period; the main focus of attention hitherto has been the larger, Protestant-owned estates. The preoccupation with the latter is understandable. Most of the land of Ireland was Protestant-owned, although that proportion, which was as high as 95 per cent in the late 18th century, declined as the 19th century progressed, especially after the Famine when several encumbered estates were bought up by Catholics, such as Nolan Ferrall himself. By 1871, 38 per cent of landlords were Catholic, but their estates were generally smaller than the Protestant-owned ones so the proportion of Catholic-owned land was probably closer to 15 per cent, which would be in line with the Catholic share of gross national rental income.[7] At that time, there were 400 landlords with estates of over 10,000 acres.[8]

The study challenges any notion that tenant hardship and landlord-tenant clashes were peculiar to the larger estates, especially those owned by absentee, Protestant landlords. On the small Logboy estate, the tenants undoubtedly suffered greatly during the Famine and probably some were evicted, albeit at a time when the estate was controlled by a receiver. Similarly, the estate was a flash point during the Land War, the Catholic determination of which tends to be exaggerated.[9] The ultimate aim of the Fenian-dominated land agitation in Mayo was the abolition of landlordism, whatever its religious hue, and in spite of the moderating views of the Catholic hierarchy about 'the just rights of landlords and of tenants'.[10] It is unclear whether Nolan Ferrall was among the many Mayo landlords who granted rent abatements in the latter half of 1879 but, in any event, that concession and the subsequent judicial rent reductions did not quell the agitation for good, even if it was temporarily dampened. For the hardliners, the agitation was less about the level of rents than about their very existence.[11]

In the course of the agitation, the small Catholic landlords such as Nolan Ferrall, his neighbour Bourke of Irishtown, the latter's cousin Walter M. Bourke of Curraghleagh, and the tenants' former advocate, P.J.B. Daly of Ballinrobe, were just as likely to be targeted – and with equal if not greater vehemence – as were their Protestant counterparts with larger estates. In fact, the smaller estates were more likely to be targeted because they were seen as more economically vulnerable and it is interesting that only four of the 'top 20' Mayo landlords, who together owned almost half the county, conceded rent abatements to their tenants in the latter half of 1879.[12] The fact that the Logboy estate was owned by Irish Catholics for over 250 years cut little ice when the crisis of 1879 occurred and the Fenian activists moved to exploit it. After two more phases of land 'war', the transition to tenant ownership was finally achieved a quarter of a century later but Nolan Ferrall did not live to see it happen.

Appendix

NOLAN FERRALL FAMILY TREE

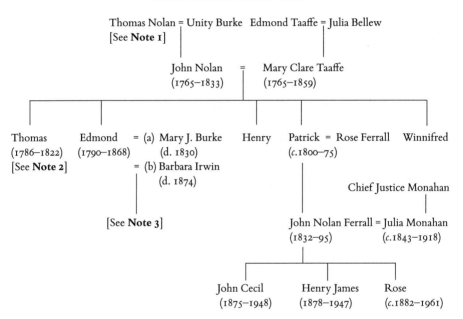

Note 1
Thomas Nolan (d. 1775) converted to Protestantism in order to retain the estate but is said to have 'lapsed to popery' just before his death.

Note 2
Thomas Nolan (1786–1822) was reputed to be the first Roman Catholic to be called to the Irish Bar after the ban on Catholics practising law was lifted by the Catholic Relief Act of 1792. His brothers, Edmond and Patrick, also entered the legal profession, as did his nephew, John Nolan Ferrall.

Note 3
Edmond Nolan and Mary Jane Burke had three children: John (1825–85), Thomas (1829–66), and Edmond (1830–48). John had 11 children, one of whom (Henry) prepared a family pedigree in 1910 tracing the family line back to Thomas Nolan (c.1555–1628) of Ballinrobe.

Notes

CSORP	Chief Secretary's Office Registered Papers
CSPS	Court Service Petty Sessions
DIB	*Dictionary of Irish biography*
HC	House of Commons
IHS	*Irish Historical Studies*
ILN	*Illustrated London News*
JGAHS	*Journal of the Galway Archaeological and Historical Society*
NAI	National Archives of Ireland, Dublin
NLI	National Library of Ireland
NHI	W.E. Vaughan (ed.), *A new history of Ireland; v, Ireland under the Union, 1801–70* (Oxford, 1989)
OS	Ordnance Survey
RD	Registry of Deeds, Dublin
RIC	Royal Irish Constabulary
TAB	Tithe Applotment Books
TNA	The National Archives, Kew, London
UIL	United Irish League

INTRODUCTION

1 Terence Dooley, *The big houses and landed estates of Ireland: a research guide* (Dublin, 2007), p. 9.

2 G.J. Lyne, *The Lansdowne estate in Kerry under the agency of William Steuart Trench, 1849–72* (Dublin 2001); Gerard Moran, *Sir Robert Gore Booth and his landed estate in county Sligo, 1814–1876: land, famine, emigration and politics* (Dublin, 2006); Anthony Doyle, *Charles Powell Leslie II's estates at Glaslough, county Monaghan* (Dublin, 2001); Joe Mooney, *The changing fortunes of the Headfort estates, 1870–1928* (Dublin, 2012); Desmond Norton, *Landlords, tenants, famine: the business of an Irish land agency in the 1840s* (Dublin, 2006).

3 J.E. Pomfret, *The struggle for land in Ireland, 1800–1923* (Princeton, 1930); E.R. Hooker, *Readjustments of agricultural tenure in Ireland* (Chapel Hill, NC, 1938).

4 Dermot James, *John Hamilton of Donegal, 1800–1884: 'this recklessly generous landlord'* (Dublin, 1998), p. x.

5 D.S. Lucey, *Land, popular politics and agrarian violence in Ireland: the case of county Kerry, 1872–86* (Dublin, 2011), p. 2.

6 Barbara Solow, *The land question and the Irish economy, 1870–1903* (Cambridge, MA, 1971).

7 J.S. Donnelly, *The land and the people of nineteenth-century Cork* (London, 1975).

8 W.E. Vaughan, *Landlords and tenants in mid-Victorian Ireland* (Oxford, 1994).

9 K.T. Hoppen, *Ireland since 1800: conflict and conformity* (2nd ed., Harlow, 1999), p. 98.

10 Norton, *Landlords, tenants, famine*, p. 321.

11 L.P. Curtis Jr, *The depiction of evictions in Ireland, 1845–1910* (Dublin, 2011), p. 129.

12 William Nolan, *Tracing the past: sources for local studies in the Republic of Ireland* (Dublin, 1982); Dooley, *The big houses*.

13 Peter Fowler and Ian Blackwell, *An English countryside explored: the land of Lettice Sweetapple* (Stroud, 1998), p. 13.

14 Raymond Gillespie and Gerard Moran, *Longford: essays in county history* (Dublin, 1991), p. 7.

15 K. Buckley 'The records of the Irish Land Commission as a source of historical evidence', *IHS*, 18:29 (Mar. 1952), 28–36.

16 L.P. Curtis, Jr, 'Incumbered wealth: landed indebtedness in post-Famine Ireland', *American Historical Review*, 85:2 (Apr. 1980), 333.

17 Recent valuable studies of west of Ireland estates include Tom Crehan, *Marcella Gerrard's Galway estate, 1820–70* (Dublin, 2013) and Michael M. O'Connor and James R. O'Connor, *When crowbar and bayonet ruled: the Land War on the Belcarra estate of Harriet Gardiner and Susanna Pringle, 1879–1910* (Dublin, 2013).

1. PRELUDE TO DISASTER: THE LOGBOY ESTATE, 1833–44

1 Rents had fallen by up to 40 per cent since 1814, according to another Mayo landlord, Thomas Linsay of Hollymount; see *Report from the Select Committee on Agriculture*, HC 1833 (612), v, 328.

2 The complexity of these settlements and the scale of charges involved are revealed in a deed dated 8 June 1816 (RD, vol. 705, pp 224–5, 483160).

3 Curtis, 'Incumbered wealth', p. 338.

4 Henry Nolan, 'Pedigree of the Nolan family of Logboy' (Hereford, 1910), hereafter cited as 'Nolan pedigree' (location of MS unknown; copy in possession of the present writer).

5 Samuel Lewis, *Topographical dictionary of Ireland* (3 vols, Dublin, 1837), i, p. 1; Edmond Nolan is listed as a subscriber.

6 James Fraser, *Guide through Ireland, descriptive of its scenery, towns, seats, antiquities, etc.* (Dublin, 1838), p. 337.

7 Application to the Commissioners for Education for a grant for a school at Logboy (or Polacapiel), Co. Mayo, dated 9 Jan. 1839 (NAI, EDI/60/103); hereafter cited as 'School grant application 1839'.

8 *Freeman's Journal*, 21 July 1836 and 23 July 1838.

9 *Freeman's Journal*, 13 May 1833.

10 'Nolan pedigree', p. 29.

11 Paul Waldron, 'The rundale system of landholding: its evolution, extinction and replacement', *South Mayo Family Research Journal* (1993), 43–56.

12 D.E. Jordan Jr, *Land and popular politics in Ireland: county Mayo from the Plantation to the Land War* (Cambridge, 1994), p. 57.

13 F.H.A. Aalen, Kevin Whelan and Matthew Stout (eds), *Atlas of the Irish rural landscape* (Cork, 1997), pp 79–88.

14 Bald's map of Co. Mayo, *c.*1813 (NLI, MS 16I/1).

15 *Report from the Select Committee on the state of Ireland: 1825*, HC 1825 (129), viii, 261.

16 Isaac Weld, *Statistical survey of the county of Roscommon* (Dublin, 1832), p. 660.

17 M.J. Molloy's 1948 play *The King of Friday's Men* features the faction-fighting at Tulrahan pattern, based on folklore he recorded from an old Tulrahan man, William Kelly.

18 Samuel Clark, *Social origins of the Land War* (Princeton, 1979), pp 73–7.

19 Aalen et al., (eds), *Atlas*, p. 88.

20 W.J. Smyth, '"Mapping the people": the growth and distribution of the population' in John Crowley, W.J. Smyth and Mike Murphy (eds), *Atlas of the great Irish famine, 1845–52* (Cork, 2012), p. 13.

21 Cormac Ó Gráda, 'Poverty, population, and agriculture, 1801–45' in *NHI*, p. 118.

22 The census data at townland level were first published in *Addenda to the census of Ireland for the year 1841* (London, 1844) but were also included, for comparison purposes, in *The census of Ireland for the year 1851, part I, showing the area, population, and number of houses, by townlands and electoral divisions, vol. iv, province of Connaught, county of Mayo*, HC 1852–53 (1542), xcii, 453; the latter is hereafter cited as 'Census report for 1851'.

23 Rental of the Nolan estate offered for sale on 7 October 1851 (NLI, Encumbered estates rentals), hereafter cited as '1851 rental'.

24 *Tenth report of the Congested Districts Board for Ireland*, HC 1901 (681), lx, 19.

25 NAI, TAB searchable database (http://titheapplotmentbooks.nationalarchives.ie/search/ tab/home.jsp.) (14 Nov. 2012).

26 Michael Comer and Nollaig Ó Muraíle (eds), *Béacán/Bekan: portrait of an east Mayo parish* (Ballinrobe, 1986), p. 190.

27 'Census report for 1851'.

28 The baptismal register for the parish of Annagh, now in local custody, records baptisms from November 1851 onwards.

29 Ó Gráda, 'Poverty', pp 122–8.

30 *Report from the Select Committee on Agriculture*, HC 1833 (612), v, 330.

31 Fr M.J. Heaney, 'Notes on Bekan Parish (Díseart Bhéacáin) compiled AD 1942', p. 52 (Tuam Diocesan Archives); hereafter cited as Heaney, 'Notes'.

32 School grant application 1839.

33 Ibid.

34 *Seventh report of the Commissioners of National Education in Ireland, for the year 1840*, HC1842 (353), xxiii, 99.

35 *Tenth report of the Commissioners of National Education in Ireland, for the year 1843*, HC 1844 (569), xxx, 109.

36 *Appendix to eleventh report of the Commissioners of National Education in Ireland, for the year 1844*, HC 1845 (650), xxvi, 96.

37 Kieran Waldron, *The archbishops of Tuam, 1700–2000* (Tuam, 2008), pp 45–8.

38 Heaney, 'Notes', pp 22–3.

39 *Freeman's Journal*, 26 July 1839.

40 Copy of 1840 lease of church site (NLI, MS D16,538).

41 *Freeman's Journal*, 18 Nov. 1840.

42 E.M. Crawford, 'Food and famine' in Cathal Póirtéir, (ed.), *The Great Irish Famine* (Dublin, 1995), p. 64.

43 *Freeman's Journal*, 26 Oct. 1842.

44 *Tuam Herald*, 13 Aug. 1842.

45 Evidence of Thomas Linsay, Hollymount, landlord, quoted in *Report from the Select Committee on Agriculture*, HC 1833 (612), v, 327.

46 Fr Bernard Durcan, parish priest of Killeadan, quoted in *Evidence taken before Her Majesty's Commissioners of Inquiry into the state of the law and practice in respect to the occupation of land in Ireland. Part II*, HC 1845 (616), xx, 389.

47 E.R.R. Green, 'Agriculture' in R.D. Edwards and T.D. Williams (eds), *The Great Famine: studies in Irish history, 1844–52* (Dublin, 1956), p. 116.

48 Ó Gráda, 'Poverty', p. 120.

49 Gerard Moran, *Sending out Ireland's poor: assisted emigration to North America in the nineteenth century* (Dublin, 2004), p. 18.

50 'Australia, N.S.W., Index to Bounty Immigrants, 1828–1842,' New South Wales State Archive, Australia (https://familysearch.org/pal:/MM9.1.1/FLKB-LYQ) (16 June 2012).

51 Bernard O'Hara, *Killasser: heritage of a Mayo parish* (Swinford, 2011), pp 49–52.

52 'Nolan pedigree', p. 11.

53 Norton, *Landlords, tenants, famine*, pp 90–3.

54 *The fifteenth report of the commissioners appointed to inquire into the duties, salaries and emoluments, of the officers, clerks, and ministers of justice, in all temporal and ecclesiastical courts in Ireland. Office of sheriff*, HC 1826 (310), xvii, 337–9.

55 Norton, *Landlords, tenants, famine*, pp 90–3.

56 *Pettigrew and Oulton's Dublin Directory, 1842*, p. 567.

57 *Freeman's Journal*, 28 Nov. 1846.

58 'Nolan pedigree', p. 30.

59 Ciarán Ó Murchadha, *The Great Famine: Ireland's agony, 1845–1852* (London & New York, 2011), p. 10.

60 Moran, *Sir Robert Gore Booth*, p. 19.

61 *Transactions of the Central Relief Committee of the Society of Friends during the Famine in Ireland, in 1846 and 1847* (Dublin, 1852, reprinted 1996), pp 10–11.

62 Cecil Woodham-Smith, *The great hunger: Ireland, 1845–1849* (London, 1962), p. 316.

63 J.S. Donnelly, 'Landlords and tenants' in *NHI*, p. 340.

64 The 1851 rental mentions the receiver 'who has been over these lands for the last seven years'.

65 W. Neilson Hancock, 'Some statistics respecting the sales of incumbered estates in Ireland', *Transactions of the Dublin Statistical Society* (2 vols, Dublin, 1851), ii, 7.

66 Evidence of Mr Kelly, magistrate and D.L. for Co. Roscommon, to the *Devon Commission*, as reported in the *Freeman's Journal*, 13 Oct. 1845.

67 P.G. Lane, 'The management of estates by financial corporations in Ireland after the Famine', *Studia Hibernica*, 14 (1974), 68.

68 Ó Murchadha, *Ireland's agony*, p. 22.

69 Jordan, *Land and popular politics*, p. 105.

70 Moran, *Sir Robert Gore Booth*, p. 33.

71 '1851 rental'.

72 *Report of the Commissioners of Inquiry into the state of the law and practice in respect of the occupation of land in Ireland*, HC 1845 (605), xix, 263.

2. THE GREAT FAMINE AND ITS AFTERMATH, 1845–75

1 *Freeman's Journal*, 15 Oct. 1845.

2 *Freeman's Journal*, 14 Nov. 1845.

3 *Potatoes (Ireland). A return of the highest price of potatoes in the various market towns in Ireland, per stone, in the week ending the 24th day of January, for the last seven years*, HC 1846 (110), xxxvii, 489.

4 Woodham-Smith, *The great hunger*, p. 104.

5 Liam Swords, *In their own words: the Famine in north Connacht, 1845–1849* (Dublin, 1999), pp 72–3.

6 Ibid., p. 81.

7 Ibid., p. 87.

8 W.J. Smyth, 'The creation of the workhouse system' in John Crowley, W.J. Smyth and Mike Murphy (eds), *Atlas of the Great Irish Famine, 1845–52* (Cork, 2012), pp 120–7.

9 Information on Castlerea workhouse is available at http://www.workhouses. org.uk/Castlerea/ (6 July 2012).

10 *Report from the Select Committee of the House of Lords on the laws relating to the relief of the destitute poor, and into the operation of the medical charities in Ireland; together with the minutes of evidence taken before the said committee*, HC 1846 (694), xi, 263.

11 *Tuam Herald*, 2 Jan. 1847.

12 Swords, *In their own words*, p. 107.

13 *Freeman's Journal*, 16 Jan. 1847.

14 *Freeman's Journal*, 15 May 1847.

15 *Mayo Constitution*, 11 Jan. 1848.

16 *Freeman's Journal*, 1 June 1847.

17 Woodham-Smith, *The great hunger*, p. 202.

18 Swords, *In their own words*, p. 309.

19 *Tuam Herald*, 30 Dec. 1848.

20 'Nolan pedigree', p. 42.

21 J.S. Donnelly, 'Mass evictions and the Great Famine: the clearances revisited' in Póirtéir (ed.), *The Great Irish Famine*, p. 159.

22 Cormac Ó Gráda, *Ireland before and after the Famine: explorations in economic history*,

1800–1925 (2nd ed., Manchester, 1993), p. 110.

23 T.H. Marshall, *Social policy in the twentieth century* (3rd ed., London, 1970), p. 19.

24 Ó Gráda, *Ireland before and after the Famine*, p. 110.

25 *Freeman's Journal*, 11 Dec. 1849.

26 *Sixteenth report of the Commissioners of National Education in Ireland.* (For the year 1849), HC 1850 (1231) (1231–II), xxv, 369.

27 *Freeman's Journal*, 3 June 1850.

28 Rental of the Nolan estate for sale on 6 July 1852 (NLI, Encumbered estates rentals).

29 Census report for 1851.

30 Ivor Hamrock (ed.), *The Famine in Mayo: a portrait from contemporary sources, 1845–50* (2nd ed., Castlebar, 2004), p. v.

31 P.G. Lane, 'The general impact of the Encumbered Estates Act of 1849 on counties Galway and Mayo', *JGAHS*, 33 (1972–73), 48.

32 Donnelly, 'Mass evictions and the Great Famine', p. 158.

33 Peter Gray, *Famine, land and politics: British government and Irish society, 1843–50* (Dublin, 1999), p. 180.

34 Donnelly, 'Landlords and tenants', p. 340.

35 Six inch OS map of 1839, Ordnance Survey Ireland, (http://maps.osi.ie) (14 Nov. 2012).

36 Desmond Norton, 'On landlord-assisted emigration from some Irish estates in the 1840s', *Agricultural History Review*, 53:1 (2005), 6.

37 *Mayo Constitution*, 15 June 1847.

38 P.G. Lane, '"Poor craythurs": the West's agricultural labourers in the nineteenth century' in Carla King and Conor McNamara (eds), *The west of Ireland: new perspectives on the nineteenth century* (Dublin, 2011), pp 42–3.

39 Nolan estate survey and maps prepared by order of the Encumbered Estates Commissioners, 1851 (MS in the possession of Eamonn Waldron, Salthill, Galway).

40 *Mayo Constitution*, 6 July 1847.

41 Joseph Lee, *The modernization of Irish society, 1848–1918* (3rd ed., Dublin, 2008), p. 6.

42 Seán O'Halloran, 'Flight from the Great Famine: the forgotten links between

Birstall (Yorkshire) and Aghamore', *Glór Achadh Mór* (2011), pp 123–9.

43 Personal email correspondence with US-based descendants of the Murrays, Aug. 2011–Dec. 2013; fortuitously, and unusually for Famine-era emigrants, it was found possible to trace the site of the ancestral Murray home because one of the Murrays placed a 'missing persons' notice in the *Boston Pilot* newspaper in 1851 which identified Cossallagh as their native townland in Ireland, while the estate map prepared that same year in connection with the sale of the Nolan estate happened to identify Thomas Murray as the previous occupier of a particular house and holding in that townland.

44 Murray gravestone in Calvary cemetery, Mapleton, Blue Earth County, Minnesota, USA (http://www.findagrave.com) (21 Nov. 2012).

45 Irish Reproductive Loans Fund Records, County Mayo, T 91/187c/0239 (TNA) (http://www.movinghere.org.uk/defaul t.htm) (16 July 2012).

46 Census returns of England and Wales, 1851, Class HO107, piece 1959, folio 79, p. 50, GSU roll 87359, (TNA) (www.ancestry.com) (16 July 2012).

47 *Vancouver Independent*, 11 May 1877.

48 Incumbered Estates Court, Ireland, *List of petitions filed from the commencement of proceedings, October 25th, 1849 to July 28th, 1853* (Dublin, 1854), p. 14.

49 Dooley, *The big houses*, p. 31.

50 1851 rental.

51 E. Keane, P. Beryl Phair and T.U. Sadlier (eds), *King's Inns admission papers, 1607–1867* (Dublin, 1982), p. 365.

52 *Freeman's Journal*, 13 Jan. 1854.

53 *Nation*, 22 Mar. 1856.

54 *Freeman's Journal*, 11 Apr. 1856.

55 *Freeman's Journal*, 17 July 1857.

56 *Freeman's Journal*, 10 Nov. 1858.

57 *Freeman's Journal*, 30 Apr. 1859.

58 *Belfast News-Letter*, 26 Apr. 1860.

59 *Thom's Irish Almanac and Official Directory for the year 1862.*

60 Heaney, 'Notes', p. 6.

61 Gus Prendergast of Culnacleha, whose father worked on the demolition of

Logboy House, quoted in *Cloonfad Parish Annual Magazine* (2001), 55.

62 Lee, *Irish society*, pp 6–8.

63 *Irish Times*, 17 Mar. 1863.

64 *Freeman's Journal*, 20 Apr. 1864.

65 Lane, 'The management of estates by financial corporations', p. 87.

66 *Freeman's Journal*, 28 Apr. 1852.

67 P.G. Lane, 'Purchases of land in counties Galway and Mayo in the Encumbered Estates Court, 1849–58', *JGAHS*, 43 (1991), 109.

68 *Freeman's Journal*, 11 Dec. 1863; 2 May 1864.

69 Rental of Nolan Ferrall estate for sale on 12 Feb. 1867 (NAI, Landed estates court rentals (O'Brien), vol. 84).

70 *Telegraph or Connaught Ranger*, 3 Sept. 1862.

71 *Freeman's Journal*, 18 Nov. 1875, reporting on the court of chancery appeal in the case of Lyons v Ferrall.

72 *Freeman's Journal*, 4 Sept. 1863.

73 *Freeman's Journal*, 29 Sept. 1863.

74 *Illustrated Australian News*, 22 Mar. 1882; the yacht was wrecked off the coast of Australia in 1887.

75 *Freeman's Journal*, 22 Mar. 1864.

76 *Irish Times*, 9 May 1865, reporting the court case in which Nolan Ferrall successfully sued the vendor of the chronometer for breach of warranty.

77 *The Times*, 29 Aug. 1864.

78 *The Times*, 11 Oct. 1864.

79 *The Era*, 8 Oct. 1865.

80 Lillie Langtry, *The days I knew* (New York, 1925), p. 33.

81 *Freeman's Journal*, 14 Mar. 1866.

82 *Tuam Herald*, 9 Mar. 1867.

83 *Freeman's Journal*, 2 Mar. 1866.

84 *Telegraph or Connaught Ranger*, 4 Nov. 1868.

85 *Irish Times*, 21 Dec. 1869.

86 Heaney, 'Notes', p. 67.

87 *Land owners in Ireland: return of owners of land of one acre and upwards in the several counties, counties of cities, and counties of towns in Ireland, showing the names of such owners arranged alphabetically in each county; their addresses, etc.* HC 1876 (1492), lxxx, 308.

88 Dooley, *The big houses*, p. 48.

89 *Freeman's Journal*, 25 June 1872.

90 *Freeman's Journal*, 24 June 1873.
91 *Freeman's Journal*, 18 Nov. 1875.
92 *Irish Times*, 19 Feb. 1876.
93 *Return of fee-simple land exposed for sale or sold in Landed Estates Court, Ireland, October 1874–76*, HC 1877 (448), lxix, 6.
94 Lee, *Irish society*, p. 68.
95 Moran, *Sir Robert Gore Booth*, pp 54–5.
96 T.W. Moody, *Davitt and Irish revolution, 1846–82* (Oxford, 1981), p.36.

3. AGRARIAN VIOLENCE: THE LAND
LEAGUE YEARS

1 Comer and Ó Muraíle (eds), *Béacán/Bekan*, p. 24.
2 Jordan, *Land and popular politics*, p. 200.
3 Petty Sessions Order Books, (NAI, CSPS, 1/1036) (www.findmypast.ie) (17 Nov. 2012).
4 Bew, *Land and the national question*, p. 57.
5 Jordan, *Land and popular politics*, pp 232–3.
6 Curtis, 'Incumbered wealth', p. 338.
7 *Return of all agrarian outrages committed in the county of Mayo, from 1st of January 1879 to 31st January 1880, giving particulars of crime, arrests, and results of proceedings*, HC 1880 (131), lx, 72.
8 Petty Sessions Order Books, (NAI, CSPS, 1/1037 (www.findmypast.ie) (26 Jan. 2014).
9 *Freeman's Journal*, 18 July 1879.
10 *Nenagh Guardian*, 21 Jan. 1880.
11 Letter dated 29 Mar. 1882 from John Nolan Ferrall to RIC Inspector General (NAI, CSORP, 1882, 23842).
12 Report dated 1 Apr. 1882 from H.D. Tyacke, RIC Sub-Inspector, Claremorris (NAI, CSORP, 1882, 23842).
13 Philip Bull, *Land, politics and nationalism: a study of the Irish land question* (Dublin, 1996), pp 96–7.
14 Moody, *Davitt*, p. 294.
15 Liam Mac Thoirdealbhaigh (ed.), *A history of Irishtown, Co. Mayo* (Irishtown, c.1990), p. 60.
16 *Freeman's Journal*, 6 Nov. 1874.
17 Jordan, *Land and popular politics*, pp 237–44.
18 Eugene Hynes, *Knock: the Virgin's apparition in nineteenth-century Ireland* (Cork, 2008), p. 151.

19 Michael Kelly, 'The Boycott link' in Comer and Ó Muraíle (eds), *Béacán/Bekan*, p. 139.
20 *Freeman's Journal*, 26 Sept. 1879, letter to the editor from John Nolan Ferrall, St. German's, Ballybrack, which elicited an alternative proposal from Mr F.H. Nash, Dublin on 10 Oct. 1879 and further correspondence culminating in a response from Nolan Ferrall on 1 Nov. 1879.
21 Petty Sessions Order Books (NAI, CSPS series) (www.findmypast.ie) (10 Aug. 2012).
22 Cancelled books for Lugboy Demesne townland (Valuation Office).
23 *The Times*, 20 Jan. 1880.
24 *Freeman's Journal*, 10 Jan. 1880.
25 *Daily News*, 17 Jan. 1880.
26 *Irish Times*, 17 Jan. 1880.
27 Glen Hooper (ed.), *The tourist's gaze: travellers to Ireland, 1800–2000* (Cork, 2001), p. 128.
28 *Freeman's Journal*, 31 Jan. 1880.
29 Dublin Mansion House Fund correspondence with Ballyhaunis/Logboy Relief Committee, Jan.–Feb. 1880 (Dublin City Archives, Ch1/52/246).
30 *Freeman's Journal*, 6 Mar. 1880.
31 *Freeman's Journal*, 3 June 1880.
32 *Freeman's Journal*, 22 Mar. 1880; *Nation*, 27 Mar. 1880.
33 *Nation*, 19 June 1880.
34 *Freeman's Journal*, 14 June 1880.
35 Gerard Moran, 'James Daly and the rise and fall of the Land League in the west of Ireland, 1879–82', *IHS*, 29:114 (Nov. 1994), 206–7.
36 *Nation*, 8 May 1880.
37 *Freeman's Journal*, 28 June 1880.
38 Gerard Moran, *A radical priest in Mayo: Fr Patrick Lavelle – the rise and fall of an Irish Nationalist, 1825–86* (Dublin, 1994), p. 171.
39 *Liverpool Mercury*, 21 Dec. 1880.
40 *Freeman's Journal*, 21 Dec. 1880.
41 *Freeman's Journal*, 30 Dec. 1880.
42 Gus Prendergast of Culnacleha, quoted in *Cloonfad Parish Annual Magazine* (2001), pp 54–5.
43 Petty Sessions Order Books (NAI, CSPS 1/1040) (www.findmypast.ie) (23 Nov. 2012).

44 *Return of Persons in Custody under Protection of Persons and Property (Ireland) Act, 1881, to March 1882*, HC 1882 (156), v, 1.

45 *Freeman's Journal*, 25 May 1881.

46 *Freeman's Journal*, 16 Sept. 1881.

47 *Nation*, 12 Feb. 1881.

48 Jordan, *Land and popular politics*, pp 293–303.

49 *Nation*, 26 Feb. 1881.

50 *Hansard*, HC 24 Mar. 1881, vol. 259, col. 1799–800.

51 *Nation*, 23 Apr. 1881.

52 *Nation*, 20 Aug. 1881.

53 *Freeman's Journal*, 15 Aug. 1881.

54 *Illustrated London News*, 19 Mar. 1881.

55 *Freeman's Journal*, 14 Sept. 1881.

56 *Connaught Telegraph*, 26 Nov. 1881.

57 Return of outrages specially reported to the Constabulary office for the year 1881 (NAI, Irish Crime Records).

58 *Connaught Telegraph*, 26 Nov. 1881.

59 The Special Commission (*The Times* v Parnell) was a judicial inquiry held in London in 1888–9 into allegations that Parnell and the Home Rule party were implicated in Land War crime.

60 *The Times*, 28 June 1889, reporting the evidence of Michael A. Waldron, Ballyhaunis.

61 *Special Commission Act, 1888: report of the proceedings before the Commissioners appointed by the Act, reprinted from The Times* (2 vols, London, 1890), i, 589.

62 Catherine Bourke Chambers, *Just a boy from home: County Mayo, Ireland* (Bloomington, IN, 2009), p. 205.

63 *Freeman's Journal*, 21 Nov. 1881.

64 Folklore recorded by the author in an interview with Johnny Lyons, Redhill, Logboy, 19 Feb. 2012.

65 Raymond Gillespie, 'And be hanged by the neck until you are dead' Introduction, in Frank Sweeney (ed.), *Hanging crimes: when Ireland used the gallows* (Cork, 2005), p. 8.

66 Lucey, *Land, popular politics and agrarian violence*, p. 198.

67 NAI, CSORP, 1881, 41845.

68 *Freeman's Journal*, 21 Nov. 1881.

69 *Irish Times*, 15 Dec. 1888.

70 RIC service record for John Turbett, 35480 (NAI, microfilm).

71 *Freeman's Journal*, 22 July 1882.

72 General register of prisoners for Richmond Gaol (www.findmypast.ie) (21 Sep. 2013).

73 NAI, CSORP, 1882, 23843.

74 M.J. Heaney, unpublished document entitled 'Sacerdotes Tuamenses' containing data on Tuam diocesan priests, *c.*1800–1965 (Tuam Diocesan Archives); thanks to Canon Kieran Waldron, Ballyhaunis, for this reference.

75 Liam Bane, *The bishop in politics: life and career of John McEvilly, bishop of Galway 1857–81, archbishop of Tuam 1881–1902* (Westport, 1993), pp 39, 101.

76 Kieran Waldron, *The archbishops of Tuam 1700–2000* (Tuam, 2008), pp 82–3.

77 Patricia Byrne, *The veiled woman of Achill: island outrage and playboy drama* (Cork, 2012), p. 19.

78 Adam Pole, 'Sheriffs' sales during the Land War, 1879–82', *IHS*, 34:136 (Nov. 2005), 386–402.

79 Minute dated 1 Apr. 1882 from HD Tyacke, Claremorris RIC and letter dated 8 Apr. 1882 from the RIC Assistant General Inspector to Nolan Ferrall (NAI, CSORP, 1882, 17892).

80 NAI, CSORP, 1882, 20082.

81 Letter dated 28 Apr. 1882 to Henry Jephson, Irish office, Great Queen St, London (NAI, CSORP, 1882, 20511).

82 Memorandum dated 3 May 1882 from Claremorris RIC (NAI, CSORP, 1882, 21485).

83 *The Special Commission Act, 1888: report of the proceedings before the Commissioners appointed by the Act, reprinted from The Times* (2 vols, London, 1890), i, 590.

84 *Irish Times*, 3 Dec. 1881.

85 Dooley, *The big houses*, p. 46.

86 Maura Cronin, *Agrarian protest in Ireland 1750–1960* (Dublin, 2012), p. 44.

4. END-GAME: 'A PEASANT PROPRIETARY'

1 K.T. Hoppen, *Ireland since 1800: conflict and conformity* (2nd ed., Harlow, 1999), p. 102.

2 Fergus Campbell, *Land and revolution: nationalist politics in the west of Ireland, 1891–1921* (Oxford, 2005), p. 16.

3 Lee, *Irish society*, p. 89.

4 Moody, *Davitt*, p. 534.

5 R.V. Comerford, 'Land war' in S.J. Connolly (ed.), *The Oxford companion to Irish history* (Oxford, 1998), p. 301.

6 Dooley, *The big houses*, p. 47.

7 *The Times*, 27 May 1882.

8 *Belfast News-Letter*, 25 Nov. 1882.

9 Curtis, *The depiction of evictions*, p. 129.

10 Christopher Clesham, 'The life and times of Walter M. Bourke' in Marie Mahon (ed.), *Claremorris in History* (Claremorris, 1987), pp 27–33.

11 Order dated 15 Oct. 1883 at Ballyhaunis petty sessions (NAI, Petty Sessions Order Books, CSPS, 1/1046).

12 *Freeman's Journal*, 20 Oct. 1883.

13 *Return of names of hundred largest ratepayers in each county in Ireland*, HC 1884–85 (219), lxvii, 47.

14 *Manchester Times*, 6 Nov. 1880.

15 *Leeds Mercury*, 15 Sept. 1883.

16 *Freeman's Journal*, 8 Nov. 1883.

17 Chief Secretary's Office internal memorandum dated 18 Sept. 1884 (NAI, CSORP, 1884, 20271).

18 Order dated 6 Aug. 1883 at Ballyhaunis petty sessions (NAI, Petty Sessions Order Books, CSPS, 1/1045).

19 *Freeman's Journal*, 25 May 1887.

20 *Connaught Telegraph*, 6 June 1885; anonymous letter to the editor.

21 *Irish Times*, 27 Nov. 1886.

22 *Tuam Herald*, 1 Jan. 1887.

23 Miriam Moffitt, *Clanricarde's planters and land agitation in east Galway, 1886–1916* (Dublin, 2011), p. 17.

24 L.M. Geary, *The Plan of Campaign, 1886–1891* (Cork, 1986), p. 21.

25 Bull, *Land, politics and nationalism*, pp 101–2.

26 Geary, *The Plan of Campaign*, p. 179.

27 RIC transcript of notes of speech made at Claremorris, Co. Mayo on 19 Jan. 1887; hereafter cited as 'RIC transcript, 1887', (NAI, transcripts of land agitation speeches prepared for the Special Commission 1888, in alphabetical order by venue, six cartons, carton ii, location 3/717).

28 'RIC transcript', 1887.

29 Geary, *The Plan of Campaign*, p. 141.

30 'RIC transcript', 1887.

31 *New Zealand Tablet*, 22 Apr. 1887.

32 *Newcastle Weekly Courant*, 21 Jan. 1887.

33 *Freeman's Journal*, 28 Feb. 1887.

34 *Ipswich Journal*, 25 Feb. 1887.

35 *Irish Times*, 26 Feb. 1887.

36 *Birmingham Daily Post*, 26 Feb. 1887.

37 Gus Prendergast of Culnacleha, whose grandmother was an eyewitness, quoted in *Cloonfad Parish Annual Magazine* (2001), pp 54–5.

38 *Freeman's Journal*, 28 Feb. 1887; *Irish Times*, 5 Mar. 1887.

39 *Aberdeen Weekly Journal*, 28 Feb. 1887.

40 *Freeman's Journal*, 22 Feb. 1887.

41 *The Times*, 31 Jan. 1889, reporting the evidence presented to the Special Commission in Jan. 1889.

42 *Tuam Herald*, 7 May 1887.

43 *Irish Times*, 31 Dec. 1887.

44 Moffitt, *Clanricarde's planters and land agitation*, p. 19.

45 *Freeman's Journal*, 21 Apr. 1891.

46 *Report on failure of potato crop and condition of poorer classes in the west of Ireland*, HC 1890–91 (131), lxiii, 20.

47 *Irish Times*, 26 July 1890.

48 *Irish Times*, 11 Jan. 1893.

49 *Freeman's Journal*, 29 Sept. 1894.

50 *Freeman's Journal*, 30 Oct. 1897.

51 Campbell, *Land and revolution*, p. 30.

52 Philip Bull, 'The formation of the United Irish League, 1898–1900: the dynamics of Irish agrarian agitation', *IHS*, 30 (2003), 414.

53 *Connaught Telegraph*, 31 May 1898.

54 *Freeman's Journal*, 9 Nov. 1898.

55 *Freeman's Journal*, 24 Oct. 1898.

56 *Connaught Telegraph*, 6–7 Dec. 1901.

57 Frank Callanan, *T.M. Healy* (Cork, 1996), p. 238.

58 Geary, *The Plan of Campaign*, p. 128.

59 *Connaught Telegraph*, 18 Jan. 1902.

60 *Connaught Telegraph*, 8 Feb. 1902.

61 Laurence Ginnell (1852–1923), land agitator and politician, became private secretary to John Dillon during the Plan of Campaign and was an unsuccessful UIL candidate for Westmeath North in the 1901 elections (*DIB*).

62 NLI, papers of John Redmond, MS 15,191/1.

63 *Freeman's Journal*, 22 Apr. 1902.

64 *Freeman's Journal*, 2 June 1902.

65 *Irish Times*, 18 Apr. 1903, reproducing reply dated 8 Apr. 1903 from William O'Brien to Patrick McDonnell, Secretary of Logboy branch UIL.

66 Sally Warwick-Haller, *William O'Brien and the Irish land war* (Dublin, 1990), pp 221–51.

67 *Irish Times*, 17 Sept. 1904.

68 *Royal Commission on Congestion in Ireland. Appendix to the ninth report. Minutes of evidence (taken in Co. Mayo, 21st August to 3rd September, 1907), and documents relating thereto*, HC 1908 (3845), xli, 530.

69 Department of Agriculture and Technical Instruction, *Banking and railway statistics, Ireland* (Dublin, 1904), pp 42–3, 46–7, 50–1.

70 Aidan Brennan (ed.), *Rolling back the years: St John's national school Logboy, 1903–2003* (Logboy, 2003), p. 17.

71 Lee, *Irish society*, p. 103.

CONCLUSION

1 Curtis, 'Incumbered Wealth', p. 334.

2 Heaney, 'Notes', p. 39.

3 The Schools' Collection, vol. 109, Logboy and Tulrahan schools (www.duchas.ie) (27 Jan. 2014).

4 Curtis, 'Incumbered wealth', p. 335.

5 Ibid., p. 361.

6 Cronin, *Agrarian protest*, p. 32.

7 W.E. Vaughan, 'Ireland *c.*1870' in *NHI*, pp 740–2.

8 Ibid., p. 759.

9 Paul Bew, *Land and the national question in Ireland, 1858–82* (Dublin, 1978), p. 217.

10 *Nation*, 12 July 1879, reproducing the text of a letter from Archbishop McHale of Tuam to Fr Michael O'Donohoe and other organizers of a tenant-right meeting at Ballyhaunis on 10 Aug. 1879.

11 Jordan, *Land and popular politics*, pp 207–8.

12 Ibid., p. 207.